# GLOBAL OPERATIONS PERSPECTIVES

Jagdish N. Sheth
Brooker Professor of Research
Graduate School of Business
University of Southern California

Golpira S. Eshghi
Associate Professor of Management
Bentley College

GN65AA
PUBLISHED BY
**SOUTH-WESTERN PUBLISHING CO.**
CINCINNATI   WEST CHICAGO, IL   CARROLLTON, TX   LIVERMORE, CA

# PREFACE

Global manufacturing and global competitiveness are often used synonymously, especially in the last ten to fifteen years. At one time, the United States was a dominant manufacturer and suddenly realized that its dominance had not been only challenged, but successfully surpassed by Japan and to some extent, by Germany.

Since manufacturing is vital to employment, taxes, and political elections, it was not surprising that governments in many countries began to pay special attention to manufacturing either for protecting the tax revenues or for developing economic incentives to attract manufacturing and operations.

Today, manufacturing and business operations are almost universally international. Not only do most of the major corporations around the world have global plants and workers, but it seems that global manufacturing impacts our everyday life: most products we buy and use have some global component whether it is in the raw materials, components, or assembled products. It is, therefore, extremely critical to understand the complexity of international manufacturing and business operations.

This volume is designed to supplement standard textbooks on production and business operations for required courses in the MBA program, as well as the advanced undergraduate level. It is intended to fulfill the accreditation requirements for internationalizing the required courses in business schools.

The volume is prepared to serve the following educational needs in production and business operations.

- It describes the forces which are encouraging global manufacturing, including improved manufacturing processes, competitive markets, government policy, and search for cost efficiency.
- It provides a strategic and managerial perspective to manufacturing and business operations.
- It investigates different strategies of global manufacturing such as exports, licenses, joint ventures, subsidiary operations, and fully integrated worldwide operations.
- It supplies an annotated bibliography which will facilitate self-study or specify projects related to international business operations.

A number of criteria were utilized in selecting the papers for this volume:

- They must be managerial in orientation.
- The authors must be well recognized for their contribution to the field.
- The authors must represent a worldwide perspective rather than strictly U.S. perspective on manufacturing and business operations.

Although the volume is designed to supplement the required production and operations courses in the MBA and the advanced undergraduate programs, it also can satisfy the needs of the Executive MBA Program, as well as corporate executive seminars on global manufacturing and business operations.

The editors and the publishers are grateful to the authors and publishers who granted permission to reprint articles included in this volume.

Jagdish N. Sheth
Golpira S. Eshghi

# CONTENTS

# INTRODUCTION

Perhaps no other area of business has recently received greater government concern and attention than manufacturing operations. Both in the United States and in many European countries, domestic manufacturing has been significantly displaced by imported products, components, and raw materials. For example, most consumer electronics marketed in the United States by such American companies as General Electric, RCA, and Zenith are manufactured abroad. This is also becoming increasingly true in the automobile industry. Chrysler has rationalized its domestic capacity to just about 40 percent of its old capacity and now buys the automobiles it markets from Mitsubishi's Japanese operations. Ford does the same thing for some of its product line by buying from Europe, Japan, and, more recently, Korea. Very large retailers such as Sears, J.C. Penney, and K-Mart also procure a significant percentage of their merchandise from foreign manufacturers.

A more significant trend in recent years has been for foreign multinationals to acquire domestic manufacturing capacity through mergers and acquisitions. For example, large chemical companies such as British Petroleum, Shell, and Hoechst have expanded their manufacturing operations in North America through acquisitions and/ or installation of new facilities. This has been equally true of Japanese companies in consumer electronics and automobiles. Toyota, Nissan, and Honda all have manufacturing operations in the United States, as do Sony and Matsushita in consumer electronics.

Since manufacturing has been historically significant to both political and fiscal policies of all levels of government (local, state, and federal), any changes in the manufacturing sector are likely to invite government concern and attention. In particular, it has become increasingly important to understand why domestic companies elect to shift their manufacturing operations overseas and why foreign companies elect to acquire or install manufacturing capacity in the domestic markets.

## Forces Driving Global Manufacturing and Operations

At least four major factors seem to be responsible for motivating companies to think of global manufacturing operations. These are summarized in Figure I.1.

Perhaps the single most important reason for pursuing global manufacturing and business operations is cost competitiveness. Since cost structures are significantly different across national boundaries, it becomes necessary to shift business operations to take advantage of differential cost structures and scale economies.

At one time, when labor was a significant cost component in manufacturing and business operations, it was necessary to shift plant capacity to countries with cheap labor including Latin America, Mexico, Taiwan, Korea, Hong Kong, and more recently Malaysia, India, and China.

Increasingly, it is *not* the cost of labor but the cost of materials and components which has encouraged companies to go abroad. For example, electronics components

**Figure I.1**

## FACTORS DRIVING GLOBAL MANUFACTURERS' OPERATIONS

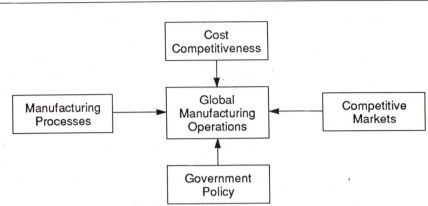

are considerably cheaper abroad, so are compressors, electrical motors, bulk chemicals, agricultural materials, and even basic metals.

Finally, transportation, shipping, tariffs, and exchange rates have become more important in shifting capacity from domestic to foreign countries. Recent decisions by Japanese companies to manufacture products such as automobiles, consumer electronics, and appliances in the United States or Canada can be directly attributed to these factors, especially the revaluation of the Japanese Yen vis-a-vis the U.S. dollar.

A second major reason for expanding manufacturing and business operations into foreign markets is due to competitive markets. For example, companies have learned that global manufacturing and marketing allows them to cross-subsidize national markets in order to gain worldwide market share and drive out competition.

Some experts believe that this was the strategy with which Michelin Tire Company entered the U.S. market and which consequently led Goodyear to retaliate by entering the European markets.

Also, as the domestic markets become mature, it becomes increasingly necessary to seek growth from international markets which eventually requires shifting capacity to those countries. For example, U.S. appliance companies, including the Whirlpool Corporation, have recently entered Latin American and Asian markets for better market opportunities. For the same reason, numerous food companies have moved rather aggressively into India, China, and more recently, the Soviet Union. Some companies, such as 3M and Motorola, have decided to expand their manufacturing capacity into foreign markets to retaliate against competitors well entrenched in those markets. Finally, new market opportunities in foreign countries also lead to international expansion of manufacturing. This is probably a good reason for AT&T, Northern Telecom, Fujitsu, and others to expand worldwide in telecommunications.

A third major force for global manufacturing is government policy. First, many countries have begun to privatize public sector industries including telecommunications, stock exchanges, health care, and mass media. This has opened up market opportunities and has consequently installed foreign manufacturing operations. Second, governments, especially in many third world countries such as India and China, have historically insisted on local manufacturing as a condition of doing business in their countries. Similarly, some governments have provided significant economic incentives to attract manufacturing from other countries in order to foster domestic economic development. For example, Ireland, Mexico, Singapore, and Malaysia have established aggressive and proactive economic development boards to attract foreign manufacturing to their countries. Finally, both changing exchange rates and tax rates have encouraged companies to distribute their manufacturing operations to hedge financial risks associated with single currency and single tax policy.

A fourth major force encouraging global manufacturing operations is improved manufacturing processes. Flexible manufacturing, computer assisted engineering, focused factories, and just-in-time processes have encouraged *distributed* manufacturing by lowering the capacity thresholds for scale economy in operations. This has resulted in microbreweries, mini-steel mills, and the worldwide manufacturing of automobiles and electronics. A second area of improved manufacturing processes is the use of information technologies (telecommunications and computers). Global networks and computerized manufacturing have reduced or eliminated time and distance barriers in many industries and consequently encouraged global operations. For example, most financial institutions (banks, brokerage, insurance) are able to do business on a global basis because of global networks. Similarly, many retailers such as Benetton are able to manufacture, store, and ship their products across many countries because of their computerized operations.

Finally, and perhaps more significantly, companies have recognized that there is an *exchange* of technology rather than a transfer of technology across national boundaries. When a U.S. company such as Ford Motor Company begins to create worldwide manufacturing to compete on a global basis, it not only transfers manufacturing technologies to Europe and Asia, but its engineers also learn from the Europeans and the Asians. This mixing of technical personnel, ideas, and expertise has proved to be invaluable in establishing world-class manufacturing. Even countries like India, Brazil, Taiwan, and China are able to teach American, European, and Japanese countries as they work together in a joint venture or a strategic alliance.

## Basic Strategies for Global Operations _____

As companies begin to expand their manufacturing and business operations across national boundaries, numerous options are immediately recognized. At the minimum, a company may decide to only export its products and not to expand its manufacturing beyond its domestic borders. This is often true in the defense industry, agriculture, and highly unique niche markets. On the other hand, a company may decide to build worldwide integrated manufacturing in which national boundaries for components, assembly, and markets are totally blurred. In such a case, it becomes difficult to label a country of origin. This seems to be increasingly true in electronics, financial services, and consulting services as well as in automobiles, pharmaceuticals, and telecommunications.

A conceptual framework that will assist a company in making global manufacturing and operations decisions is illustrated in Figure I-2. Figure I-2 summarizes the framework and the basic options available to a company. In this conceptual framework, the twin determinants of global operations are capacity rationalization and localization of operations.

Capacity rationalization reflects issues associated with efficiency of operations. In general, excess capacity, redundant operations, and scale economics will determine whether capacity rationalization is necessary or desirable. For example, many competitors expand capacity in anticipation of market growth, develop redundant operations, and are often operating at a scale where each one is inefficient. Therefore, it is not uncommon for the two competitors to merge their operations in order to rationalize them. Indeed, this is the only way each one can survive profitably. Recently, we have witnessed these types of mergers and acquisitions in the airlines, processed foods, soft drinks, and electronics, both within a country and across national borders.

Localization of operations may be necessary for a number of reasons. Technical standards may vary from country to country, this is especially true in telecommunications and computers. Governments may mandate or encourge localization of operations due to employment, education, and other national goals, as is often true in many third world countries. Finally, market characteristics including cultural and climatic conditions may warrant localization of operations. For example, McDonalds has felt that its operations must be localized within a country to accommodate cultural and climatic differences in fast foods.

If neither the capacity rationalization nor the localization of operations is important in doing business internationally, then export operations is the best option. It is likely that the product is generic, shipping cost is not critical, and domestic manufacturing is efficient for export purposes. This is often the case for cut diamonds. It is also true for basic materials which have high value-to-weight ratios such as gold, silver, and other precious or strategic metals.

**Figure I.2**

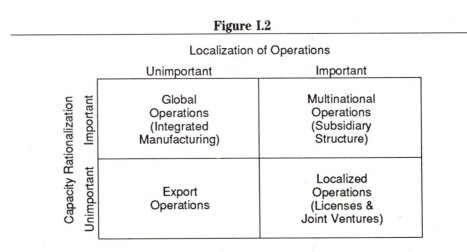

| | | Localization of Operations | |
| --- | --- | --- | --- |
| | | Unimportant | Important |
| Capacity Rationalization | Important | Global Operations (Integrated Manufacturing) | Multinational Operations (Subsidiary Structure) |
| | Unimportant | Export Operations | Localized Operations (Licenses & Joint Ventures) |

If capacity rationalization is not important but localization of operations is important for any of the reasons explained earlier, the best manufacturing option is localized operations through licensing or joint ventures. This is often prevalent in specialty chemicals, telecommunications, and processed foods.

On the other hand, if both capacity rationalization and localization of operations are critical in an industry, it is probably desirable to set up subsidiary operations. These subsidiaries are controlled and managed by the company and have both operational and managerial interdependence for efficiency purposes. For example, this is often prevalent in the appliances industry where product customization by country or region is often necessary, but at the same time there are significant scale economies especially with respect to the interchangeable parts or components of the product. The same seems to be true in many professional services such as advertising agencies, public accounting, and consulting services.

Finally, when rationalization of capacity is extremely important and localization of operations is not critical, it is best to move toward global operations through integrated manufacturing. This is becoming increasingly true in consumer electronics, office equipment, and in commercial aviation. One would expect localization of operations to become less important as Europe moves towards full economic integration and as the United States and Canada agree to economic integration in the near future. In many industries, through GATT negotiations, the United Nations, and other world agencies, there has been a movement toward establishing worldwide standards. This is emerging in telecommunications, for example. In those instances, we should expect global operations and integrated manufacturing.

## Book Summary

The book is organized into four parts. The first part focuses on the environment which is likely to shape international manufacturing and operations. A number of factors are likely to encourage global production operations and rationalization of worldwide capacity. These include product market maturity and consequent price competition, transshipment and transportation cost efficiencies as compared to manufacturing experience curves, and in general, changing economics of manufacturing. It will become increasingly difficult to convince subsidiary managers in different countries that rationalization of capacity and the development of integrated manufacturing are essential.

Part Two of the book focuses on manufacturing strategies. It discusses strategies for regaining manufacturing competitiveness, especially by the U.S. companies. This can be achieved by shifting the management philosophies developed in the early 1900s to more contemporary approaches to workforce management. For example, Taylor's scientific management principle, which suggests workers ought to be told what to do, needs to evolve toward a participative management philosophy embodied in such concepts as quality circles and worker councils. This section also discusses global manufacturing strategies evolving among the American, European, and Japanese companies, as manufacturing technologies rely more and more on computers and robotics as well as statistical process quality control. For example, while both the U.S. and the European companies use modern manufacturing techniques for improved product quality and rapid delivery, Japanese companies are using them to obtain lower prices and rapid product development.

The third part of the book discusses specific manufacturing practices around the world. It describes Japanese manufacturing practices and what the rest of the world can learn from them. For example, bias toward action, rapid tool-setting, small lot production, and mixed assembly production concepts, all prevalent in Japanese companies, may not be easy to transfer because of corporate culture and structure barriers. The section also discusses the strategic importance of information technologies and quality circle philosophy in manufacturing.

The last section of the book consists of several special topics which are directly or indirectly related to global manufacturing operations. One such topic is the critical role of supplier relationships and procurement procedures in just-in-time operations. Another article discusses why vertical integration is not very useful or efficient in today's competitive business as contrasted with early days of manufacturing.

The book provides an annotated bibliography of references which may be useful to the student for further research and readings.

# I ———— ENVIRONMENTAL ISSUES ————

# 1. GLOBAL PRODUCTION AND OPERATIONS STRATEGY

## MARTIN K. STARR

*Martin K. Starr is Professor of Management Operations and Director of the Center for Operations at Columbia University Graduate School of Business. He has authored or coauthored numerous books and papers dealing with production and operations management and management science. His current teaching and research interests are management science applied to complete systems, operations management, and productivity.*

This article provides an exposition of the strategic considerations important to the development of a successful global production operation. A global network model is developed which lists the dimensions of factors providing comparative advantages in international markets.

New competitive pressures exist for normally nationally-constrained (domestic) enterprises to innovatively engage in global production operations. Why is this so? First, new technologies that lower operating costs require greater capital investment. To pay for the increased investments, greater sales volumes are essential. Since many countries have far smaller domestic consumer markets than the US, they must compete abroad to achieve sales that justify the large investments. This is particularly true when competition at home (say in Japan) is greater than in other countries, like the US. The global competing companies set standards that the domestic producers must match. As they raise their standards to compete at home, these domestic producers recognize the advantages of adopting global strategies. Second, various governments support their export industries with industrial policies that make them highly competitive so that their trade balances can be very profitable.

Third, the global setting has produced international suppliers with advantages over domestic vendors. Fourth, it has increased the volume of goods shipped, which has lowered the costs of distribution. This can provide marginal advantages to those engaged in high-volume, long-distance distribution which often circumvents union and governmental regulations. Fifth, global firms can enjoy the fluctuation of exchange rates, inflation rates and other volatile factors that provide advantages precisely because they do fluctuate, if they know how to benefit from the ups-and-downs. Volatility of fundamental economic factors challenges those who rely on stability and provides great opportunities for those who do not build strategies based on stability. For simplicity, we can assume that the production operations are associated with manufacturing. However, much of what we say in this article applies to services as well. For example, consider McDonald's which makes and sells hamburgers in many parts of the world. This productline and its packaging are about as different from

Martin K. Starr, "Global Production and Operations Strategy," *Columbia Journal of World Business* 19.4 (Winter 1984): 17–22. Reprinted by permission.

computers and software as one can imagine. Nevertheless, comparisons can be drawn between the way McDonald's does its global thing, and say IBM. The IBM pattern of manufacture has high local content in a great variety of countries, but production of components is not constrained to be exclusive, and transfers occur between countries. The study of many companies reveals great strategic differences between them, in how they allocate the global resources, and for each company incessant, dynamic, evolutionary change, reflecting opportunities to innovate.

## What is Global Production? _____

The definition of global production is not cut and dried. Variability of product design to satisfy each country's UL (Underwriting Laboratory) requirements, different food and drug regulations, and even national taste anomalies, create complexities that lead to questions of how many factories make sense, and where they should be located. Decisions to license, export or produce within foreign country are clear choices of different global strategies. When mixed together, they comprise so great a potential number of combinations across many countries, that ordinary rationality is challenged and defeated.

Production management includes distribution, although in such applications it is often called operations management (OM). The OM designation is also used for process management in banking, transportation and other services, as well as for managing services that support manufacturing operations. World-wide distribution systems provide an excellent example of global operations. Specialized carriers can significantly alter the direct costs of goods sold and delivered to customers. Toyota, for example, has shown that when export volume warrants the investment, ships specially designed to carry automobiles from plant to market can efficiently provide a strategic advantage that affects the decision of where to manufacture, *how much* to produce, and destined for *which* markets.

Also to be included in global production strategy is the issue of global sourcing. Who can be chosen to supply raw materials and components to a manufacturer is clearly a function of who that manufacturer considers to be part of the list of potential vendors. In the past, regional (and at most, national) familiarity led to "safe" decisions, meaning comfortable with the language and culture of the supplier. But now, options that are reasonable (and/or essential) to consider exist all over the world. Supplier selection must be dictated by analyses of comparative factor advantages of cost, quality, variety, service, delivery, warranties, reliabilities and flexibilities. Competitive advantages as they appear in the factor list are derived from superior technology, methodology and management. More specifically, there are lots of factors that contribute to comparative advantage, for example, lower labor costs, higher worker skills, more favorable exchange rates, better lead times for delivery including carriers' reliability; and less danger of supply interruption through vendor or carrier strikes, etc. As risk exposure increases, multiple vendor selection becomes a necessity. Thus, with the vendor selection menu being global in scope, and growing, this aspect of the production problem allows unique opportunities for innovating to achieve competitive advantages.

## Global Life Cycle Factors ───────────────────────────────────────────

A manufacturer, with a strictly domestic market, deciding to order from a vendor located in another country—and this for the first time—may acquire information which then leads to the development of new markets abroad. Suppliers of manufactured goods can ship components or finished goods. The latter, as exporters, need no intermediate fabrication or assembly locations outside of their home base. Eventually, export strategies can change to plans to manufacture in that export country, with imports of at least some components from home base. Alternatively, by licensing the production process, fabrication and assembly can be conducted in the country which previously had been supplied by export. But licensing has a contractual end-date, at which time, the best decision may have changed to plant ownership abroad.

These are a few of the many dynamic systems that have to be reviewed continuously, with the distinct likelihood of major capital investment reconfiguration decisions. The reason is that country economics, industry concentrations, technological improvements and consumer markets change with age and experience, in what are aptly called "life cycles". Such life cycles have always been around, but, for global systems, they are more volatile waves of greater volume that are speeded up by various new forces.

First, more countries, with their own governmental support, introduce new players in the competitive global game. On a broader canvas, national economies world-wide are experiencing faster and broader change than ever before.

Second, industry concentrations are significantly altered by global producers and marketers who cross national boundaries. Worldwide, a greater number of producers have assembled increasingly larger aggregate volumes as a result of their global activities. This translates into more competition between companies having better production processes, yielding higher quality and lower costs for consumers. These benefits start dissipating when governmental regulations are invoked to protect domestic producers. Protecting domestic producers increases concentrations and decreases competition and consumer benefits. However, increasingly, tariffs and quotas have shifted global marketing efforts into production investments inside the protected zone. The domestic proponents of protectionism find themselves (unexpectedly) involved in greater competition. They must invest in improvements of their production systems to match the competition.

Third, technological change, driven by semiconductor capacity and circuit design developments, decreasing computer costs and growing software intelligence, have no historical counterpart with respect to their impact and rate of change. Worldwide, individual governments are sponsoring research. Such R&D accomplishments cannot be overlooked, although their effects upon the global market are significantly less now than they will become in the future.

Fourth, with more options to choose from, especially as induced by global competition among technologically vaulting countries, consumers shorten product lives faster than ever.

There is a fifth point to be treated, as well. New technology alone is not responsible for the dynamics of life cycles. Global production systems have been unique in the extent to which they reflect changed process configurations and management principles. The Japanese model of management (job rotation, lifetime security, worker production-goal bonuses, consensus, etc.) has received major coverage by business publications.

Only slightly less journalistic attention has been paid to production techniques and procedures which include JIT (Just-in-Time), Kanban (cards) for production scheduling and TQC (Total Quality Control) with workers organized in Quality Circles.

## Global Network Models _____

Ricardo (about 1800) formulated the notion of comparative advantage to explain international trading patterns. (An updated simplistic example: OPEC countries export oil and import autos from the countries that need oil to produce and export cars.) Nationally-owned physical resources dominate this early viewpoint, but trade-offs with technological know-how do occur. Cost advantages are the primary focus, although some generalized quality standards and reliable delivery lead times must be assumed. Ricardo's insights still apply, but what constitutes comparative advantage for global firms engaged in international trade has taken on many new dimensions.

The point to be made is that sourcing, fabricating, assembling and distributing decisions are becoming increasingly interdependent and critical in terms of the differences available between the best, the average, and the worst, with respect to: costs, quality, variety, service, deliveries, warranties, reliabilities and flexibilities. The global environment contributes significantly to the dimensional enrichment of what constitutes comparative advantage. As some examples:

- increasing numbers of international suppliers appear with technological advantages in production processes, distribution (delivery) systems, and warehousing methods,
- new technology factories become feasible that (sometimes) can be installed abroad more easily than at home—this is because of many reasons, including union/management difficulties, national regulations, and lack of domestic competition that can match the global incursions,
- high-tech assembly systems can be installed in various parts of the world using computer software that can be created in one country and then shipped to the others; modifications can originate anywhere and go everywhere else; remote entry programming via satellite is not only economically feasible, it may be nearing optimality. Such computer control applies to new technology (fabrication) factories as well.

The model that allows total consideration of global sourcing, making, assembling and marketing (including distribution) alternatives is that of a network, as shown in Chart 1.

The network is a rational expression of all possible combinations of the hierarchical chain of supply and demand which starts with raw materials and ends with markets. Not all possible connections (links) are drawn between the (nodes) suppliers, fabricators, assemblers and marketers, but they all could be drawn and considered.

## Chart 1
### CONSIDERS MOST POSSIBLE COMBINATIONS

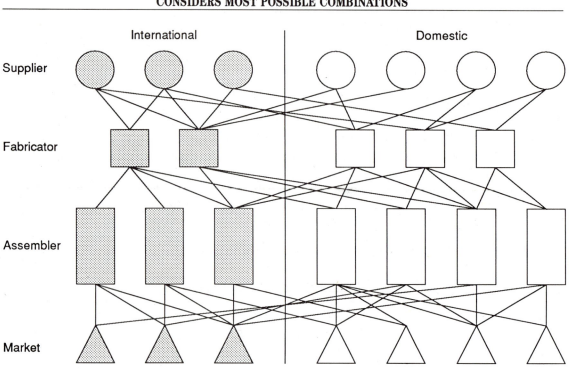

The reason for considering less than all possible combinations is that constraints exist which may be real or imaginary. For example, it should be noted that a strictly domestic arrangement might look as shown in Chart 2. In any case, management seldom wishes to allow all possible options. Further, the list of existing suppliers, factories and markets provides a foundation to which other nodes can be added. If you don't know about a potentially important new supplier in Korea, you can't add that node to the network; once known, you will add it.

The means of solving these complex network models exist, assuming that the costs and benefits can be determined. The costs, in most instances can be catalogued for various suppliers. However, global sourcing involves an exchange rate interface, which is difficult to predict because it is volatile and subject to many forces that transcend single company or even industry-wide knowledge.

Inflation rates differ by nations which can also affect purchasing as well as producing and marketing decisions. Sometimes good predictions of inflation rates are easy to come by; namely, when the rates of change are fairly constant over time. When this is not the case, and with exchange rate volatility, many decisions are made irrationally. Yet, in every spin of the roulette wheel, some players win. And, for those who know more about such subjects, knowledge of the past plus sound intuition may provide substantial leverage.

The use of a global network model requires global market data which is needed to determine the marginal contribution of total revenues less total production costs.

## Chart 2
### A STRICTLY DOMESTIC ENTERPRISE IS SHOWN BY SOLID FILLED-IN NODES

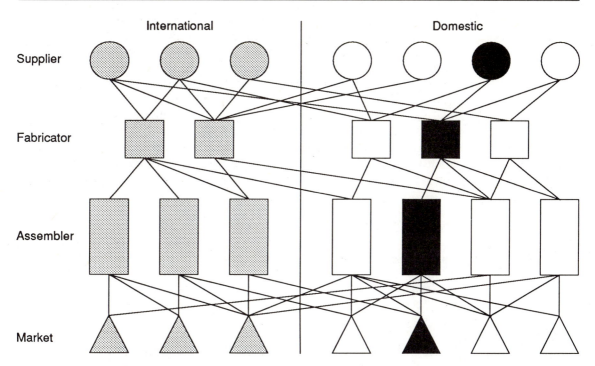

Such figures are somewhat less difficult to estimate on a global scale if there exist national markets for each production subsidiary. Problems of translating quality into costs and benefits, are another example of difficulties encountered in using models. However, there are tricks which take us a good distance of the way, and in this instance sensitivity analysis which tests performance for different levels of costs and benefits, provides insights concerning the effects of quality levels. So, in general, while we have emphasized measurement problems, we have also noted that they are not insuperable. By chance, there will be winners and losers. By skill, the probabilities of winning can be increased manyfold.

## Transportation and Transshipment Models _____

The transportation model is a simple way of determining the optimal pattern of shipping from a set of origins to a set of destinations. This could be from a list of potential suppliers (global and domestic) to existing as well as potential production facilities (global and domestic) as represented by the top two levels of Chart 1. It could also be from fabricators (say domestic only) to assembly plants in strategic international locations. In many instances, the fabricators and assemblers would be located in the same plant. However, when the transportation costs of moving finished goods to the marketplace are high, (as in automobiles) it is not unusual to locate assembly plants near the market. This would alter Chart 1 as shown in Chart 3. In this case, the company's own production facilities become alternative (or constrained) suppliers to the assembly operations. The costs and benefits derived for the transportation model, where origins are assemblers and destinations are markets, clearly influences the location decisions for suppliers, company fabrication plant (and even subassembly plants, say for auto engines, to provide a realistic example), assembly plants and targeted markets.

To capture the entire 4-tier hierarchy in the network requires a modification of the transportation model which is called a transshipment model.[1] It encompasses the total network, i.e., suppliers to (fabrication and assembly) producers, to markets. A simple alteration of the well-known transportation model, takes care of the more complicated situation. We will not deal with the mathematics of solving the transportation or the transshipment problem in this paper. Every major computer company has soft-ware that works for sizeable problems.

## Competitive Advantage

Innovation does not have to originate in-company. Finding supplier innovations, anywhere in the world, is a new responsibility which many organizations cannot yet meet. In the past decade, competitive analysis has been adopted by many companies,

## Chart 3
### SUPPLIER CAN SHIP DIRECTLY TO ASSEMBLERS

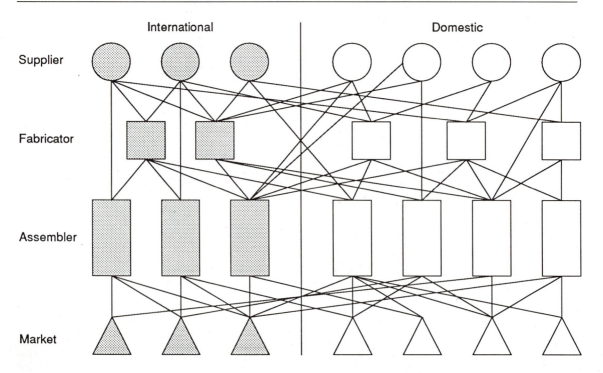

and perfected by a few. The focus was on the market. Substitutability in the consumers' minds for "what they will buy" defined competition. As the global perspective emerged, it became clear that competitive advantage included more than marketing. Zenith Radio, in the 1960s, scrutinized RCA and GE. By the 1970s, RCA and Zenith were looking abroad, studying Sony's products, and Panasonic's, etc. Now, in the mid-1980s, these companies no longer look only at each other. They also look to alternative:

- raw material suppliers
- machine tool and other process technology suppliers
- component suppliers
- arrangements with co-producers
- R&D sources (see Chart 4)
- other opportunities for unique basic advantages (called UBA's)

## The Effects of New Tech, New Production Theory and New Management Principles _____

Previously, companies located their production facilities in line with many established rational principles. One of the most significant forces for global production was to assemble sufficient marketing volume to permit a large production facility to be built

**Chart 4**

**GLOBAL VIEWS OF R & D CAN ORIGINATE FROM DOMESTIC AND/OR INTERNATIONAL SOURCES**

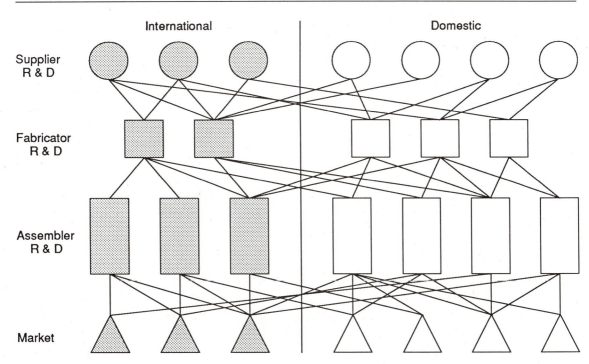

which could reflect economies of scale that were inherent in the manufacturing process.

Now, in an increasing number of industries there exists profoundly new technology known as FMS (Flexible Manufacturing Systems). FMS has altered established production theory by using tools and transfer lines operated by computer software that can produce many different designs in low volumes (often 1 at a time) with exceptionally high quality. The investment is high, but it yields production configurations with the same economies of scale as formerly achieved by the large volume producers who could only produce a single output. Thus *economies of scope* can become more important in providing UBA's than economies of scale which no longer dominate all production investment decisions. The key to understanding these changes is the ability of new technology to achieve near-zero set-up times and cost.

In the purest cases, many FMS factories can be built in different countries to comply with local content pressures—whether regulated or just bowing to social pressures. Assembly operations are moving in the same direction, and many industries are finding ways to shift their local content.

The key differences are based on ways to reduce waste. Work in process (WIP) must be brought to a minimum level. Defectives can be decreased by using the total quality control concept. Just in time deliveries by suppliers is an external criterion that requires special relations between vendors and users. Managers begin to work with employees to continually improve the production process. Especially, the effort is to drive set-up costs to near zero, while improving quality.

When all is in place, optimal producers emerge. They have the comparative advantage of achieving maximal margin contribution both short- and long-term. Opportunities for innovation at a strategic level have never been greater. The crucial variables belong to production and operations strategies.

In summary, if national companies want to survive and remain competitive they must look at global opportunities—because if they don't do this others are already getting ready to grab their markets with superior strategies that include lower costs, sharper market penetration in quality and design variability and better distribution. Global networking is crucial for gaining the competitive edge.

## Note

1. Transshipment problem is a transportation problem that is modified to allow either supply or demand points to serve as transshipment points, receiving units that are to be eventually shipped elsewhere. From Dannenbring and Starr, *Management Science: An Introduction,* 1981, pp. 347–349.

## References

David G. Dannenbring and Martin K. Starr, *Management Science: An Introduction,* McGraw-Hill Book Company, NY, 1981.

Subhash C. Jain and Louis R. Tucker, Jr., *International Marketing: Managerial Perspectives,* CBI Publishing Co., Inc., Boston, MA.

John D. Daniels, et al., *International Business: Environments & Operations* (3rd ed.), Addison-Wesley Publishing Co., 1952.

Michael F. Porter, *Competitive Strategy,* Free Press, NY, 1980.

# 2. MANAGING MANUFACTURING RATIONALIZATION WITHIN MULTINATIONAL COMPANIES

## YVES L. DOZ

*Yves L. Doz is an Assistant Professor at Harvard Business School. He was trained at the Ecole des Hautes Commerciales in Paris and at Harvard. He is currently doing research on the relations between national governments and multinational corporations.*

Reduction of tariffs and other trade barriers and the emergence of free trade areas in Western Europe have provided an opportunity to multinational companies (MNC's) manufacturing in several countries to have each of their plants specialize and ship production to other subsidiaries for sale or integration into finished products. Instead of multiproduct-multistage plants autonomously serving a national market, it has become feasible and economically attractive to develop plants that manufacture only one model or one product line, or are involved in only certain stages of the production process for the worldwide market.

Rationalization means shifting from a set of local-for-local plants, each serving its own national market with a broad product range, to an integrated network of large-scale production-specialized plants serving the world market. Only a few products, or some components, are made in each plant, but in very large numbers. Rationalization also involves the development of a single worldwide product line and the integrated management of product engineering activities to avoid duplications and to maintain production specialization.

Not all companies can benefit equally from rationalizing their production. In some cases transportation costs would be disproportionate; in others, economies of scale beyond the current plant sizes do not warrant rationalization; in still others, customers' tastes and preferences differ sufficiently between countries to jeopardize any attempt to rationalize. Nevertheless, many companies, with less-differentiated products where economies of scale are important and where making a full line of sizes or models or types is critical for successful competition, can derive immense benefits from rationalization, particularly when their production costs are important in relation to total costs.

For mature industries in developed countries, rationalization must be seriously considered. Multinationals face more and more competition from Japan, whose industry is very efficient; from lesser developed countries who have lower labor or energy costs; and from competitors who do not follow usual trade practices or pricing policies (e.g., the Soviet bloc). Given the extreme concern that governments show

Yves L. Doz, "Managing Manufacturing Rationalization Within Multinational Companies," *Columbia Journal of World Business* 13.3 (Fall 1978): 82–94. Reprinted by permission.

toward maintaining employment, a multinational can hardly shrink its activities in developed countries and move them to lower cost countries without social upheavals that can damage its prospects permanently. The issue then often becomes how to increase production efficiency in order to maintain or restore competitiveness. Probably the greatest untapped source of efficiency is rationalizing production (and often product engineering) activities between several countries.

Despite its economic advantages, rationalization seldom is implemented as part of a new opportunity-seeking strategy. Rather, it emerges as a response to serious difficulties. According to a survey[1] taken in 1974, a number of years after trade barriers were reduced, few of the companies who had been expected to rationalize their manufacturing operations had done so. In many cases companies had invested into new subsidiaries abroad rather than serve foreign markets through exports. Only in a few industries that were subjected to very severe Far Eastern competition had multinationals rationalized their European operations. And, even then, the process of rationalization was often slow, difficult, and not always successful. Most managers attributed the difficulties of the rationalization process to administrative and managerial issues that made implementation difficult. There was no dearth of analytical studies calling for rationalization, but few of them had been followed by actual implementation.

## Rationalization: Necessary But Difficult to Diagnose _____

This paper, based on clinical research into the management of a number of large diversified MNC's over the last two years, proposes a framework for diagnosing the need for rationalization and for managing the rationalization process. The paper first suggests how to determine whether a MNC should rationalize production and what difficulties are likely to interfere with an objective diagnosis; it then analyzes problems of implementation and suggests administrative measures that can facilitate the rationalization process.

The difficulties of rationalization begin when analytical and behavioral issues conflict. The purely analytical issues are simple: rationalization is needed when product market maturity leads to price competition and product standardization on a worldwide basis. Rationalization is possible when product unit costs are sensitive to scale of manufacture, i.e., when longer series or larger plants result in lower unit costs.

Yet, social and political difficulties within the multinational corporation often hinder an objective diagnosis and delay the start of rationalization. If we pause to consider the structure of the MNC prior to rationalization, the difficulties become clear. In all likelihood the relative self-sustenance of national subsidiaries primarily geared to their domestic market has led over time to separate management of the various national companies. In such a fragmented setting there are obvious barriers to the emergence of multicountry rationalization as a strongly supported proposal. First, the significance of new competition is often difficult to recognize rapidly. Second, the decentralized management characteristic of local-for-local operations make national managers look for local-for-local solutions first. Finally, because rationalization threatens their power and identity, managers approach it with great reluctance.

## Table 1
## A FRAMEWORK FOR MANAGING THE RATIONALIZATION PROCESS

| Diagnosis | Start-up | Changes in The Management Process | Corporate Management Options To Support Rationalization |
|---|---|---|---|
| Product Market Maturity | Product Type Inventory Coordination Group | Marketing Coordination Export Coordination | Communication of Purpose Planning Integration |
| Price Competition | Staff Experts | and Sourcing Control | Changes in Measurement, |
| Unexploited Scale Economies | Coordinators | Logistics Overall Market Share Production Programming Technical Coordination Funding: R&D, Capital | Evaluation and Reward Systems Changes in Career Paths and Management Development |

| Pitfalls | | | |
|---|---|---|---|
| Lack of Perception of New Competition | Too Assertive Coordinator | Wrong Timing Inappropriate Sequencing | Lack of Top Management Visible Support |
| Autonomous Subsidiary Structure Favors National Responses Rather than Rationalization Need Diagnosis | Too Little Top Management Support to Coordinators Coordinators Subordinate to Group of Subsidiary Managers | Poor Choice of Coordinators | Continuation of Country-Based Evaluation and Compensation Schemes Poor Choice of Country Managers |
| Rationalization May Be Opposed by National Subsidiary Managers' Slanted Diagnosis | Too Many Subsidiaries Joint Ventures | | |

## Product Market Maturity and Price Competition _____

Rationalization is most needed in mature industries whose customers use precise, hard criteria based on product price performance relationships in their purchasing decisions. For instance, European consumers have developed an increasingly discriminating attitude toward cars and hi-fi sets since the 1950s; they now require high quality, low price, no-nonsense products. The same tendency is seen in the

U.S. computer industry where, as products have matured and become better known, customers have become more price sensitive. In response to customers' shifts, suppliers can put more emphasis on cost reduction rather than product differentiation or new innovative products. Product innovations become harder to come by because most aspects of the technology, functions and possible variations of the product itself have already been explored by one competitor or another. Innovative efforts are now geared to low cost production processes rather than new products.[2]

Such conditions usually lead competitors to strive for low production costs through extensive rationalization in high cost areas, through sheer size, and through production in lower cost countries. Warning signals to MNC's in developed countries can come from low cost imports taking a growing market share in home markets, other MNC's rationalizing their activities, or large scale national producers exporting aggressively. When such signals appear, rationalization is usually urgently needed or profits may soon tumble. In the free trade environment of the western world, products such as cars, trucks, bearings, electrical motors, and consumer electronics are obvious candidates for rationalization.

## Economics of Manufacture

Rationalization can bring great benefits only if the production process is highly sensitive to scale economies. Although there are no fast rules, it is generally accepted that production cost decreases depend on two major variables:

1. The size of a given operation. A 500,000 unit per year capacity automobile plant will have lower unit costs than, say, a 200,000 unit per year plant, for example.[3]
2. The number of units produced by a given operation since it started, i.e., accumulated experience.[4] To some extent this applies both to particular products (i.e., Volkswagen production) and to more general experience in a given industry (refrigerator real costs fall for any given manufacturer, with a product range evolving over time).

An analysis of the sensitivity of unit costs to scale of production is a key part of diagnosing a need for rationalization. If higher production volumes will yield much lower production costs, rationalization is highly desirable. As much as feasible, one must be careful (particularly for multiproduct, multistage-related activities) to identify what cost decreases derive from longer individual production series, overall accrued experience, or sheer size of the plant, as these differences imply different rationalization patterns. For instance, in consumer good production, audio products are easier to rationalize than video products. Radio and hi-fi production costs are mostly sensitive to individual production series, of which there are many different types. Existing small plants in various countries can specialize without too much difficulty. In TV tube production, on the other hand, there are few types and individual plants need to be very large; hence, it is very difficult for a large number of existing plants to specialize without many factory closings that are, at best, difficult and slow to implement in most developed countries.

Furthermore, more efficient manufacturing processes often require larger production volumes in a single site to reach their full efficiency. For instance, a variety of ball bearings can be produced on the same set of machines, each type in relatively small numbers. Bearings can also be produced on highly efficient fully automated transfer lines. Each line produces only one type, but in extremely large quantities. Concentrating all production of one type in one location often permits the adoption of more efficient production processes leading immediately to a spectacular drop in manufacturing costs. This was a key to SKF's rationalization success within its five main European subsidiaries.

Finally, economies of scale can affect various stages in the production process differently. Some stages can be very scale sensitive (for instance wafer production in semiconductors), others very labor intensive but not much affected by scale (semiconductor packaging), still others both scale sensitive and labor intensive (semiconductor testing). These differences are reflected by the patterns of production rationalization of the U.S. semiconductor companies: wafer manufacture in very large plants in the U.S., assembly and packaging farmed out to the Far East and Latin America, and testing in various locations.

## Potential Pitfalls in Diagnosis

In an analytical perspective, diagnosing the need for rationalization is relatively simple; product standardization and price competition in mature product markets and the existence of further economies of scale are the key elements. Why, then, is diagnosis so difficult to carry out? Information difficulties may delay the perception of new competition, national subsidiary autonomy makes a worldwide diagnosis most difficult, and national managers see rationalization cutting across their power base.

### Information Difficulties

It is difficult to detect an overall threat to the company's competitive position. Acute competitive pressure are seldom felt in all countries simultaneously. New, low price competitors adopt a gradual approach, seldom storming a whole continent at once. They may strike first where established manufacturers have lesser stakes, as did the importers of Japanese cars in Europe by first penetrating countries such as Belgium, Denmark or Portugal, where no home-based European manufacturer felt the pinch immediately. Delays in building distribution networks and a fragmented users' market may further blur the perception of new competition.

The company itself is often in a poor position to detect overall competitive pressures. Over the years, predominance of a national orientation can lead to decay of central management. Lean (or sometimes non-existent) corporate staffs, the absence of systematic exchange of information about specific products and markets between national subsidiaries, and the lack of worldwide product management all add to the difficulties of synthesizing a global view of competitors from the fragmentary glimpses provided by the subsidiaries.

### Structural Difficulties

Often the wide-ranging operational decentralization granted to national subsidiary managers is compensated with tight profit and loss accountability. Such a control mechanism reinforces the desire of a national subsidiary manager to feel responsible and usually prompts him to reach for solutions he can first implement by himself. Faced with deteriorating profits, he is more likely to react by cutting costs and trimming employment that he can control than by calling for a companywide strategic and structural change.

Furthermore, the national subsidiary structure favors the development of commitments by managers. Other researchers[5] have shown the importance of these commitments in delaying and weakening management intervention into crisis situations, and in stalling strategic changes. A firm belief, shared by a whole organization, that operational responsibility and accountability are better placed at the national level, is difficult to change. This is particularly true of European top managers whose formative years witnessed a breakdown of international relations (protectionism in the Great Depression, immediately followed by World War II) and who may be reluctant to take advantage of conditions of free trade which they regard as vulnerable and of institutions they consider fragile (the EEC administrative and regulatory machinery).

Such beliefs are sometimes reinforced by the incomplete state of free trade. In some industries, scale economies of production and price competition would dictate rationalization but the strategic importance of the products prompts national governments to prevent or limit international trade and rationalization of production, as with telecommunication equipment and electrical power systems.[6] In some other cases employment considerations or technological and financial factors prompt governments to prevent rationalization, through financial incentives, export subsidies, research grants, and other benefits, made contingent upon full local production. For many industries the extent of rationalization may thus be informally limited by national subsidiary managers who are more attuned to the possible national government desires for full local production than to the benefits of rationalization.

Delegation of responsibility to the national level may prevent top management from developing a clear-cut overall proactive view of the evolution of the company in response to worldwide competition. Without a will to develop global strategies for dealing with the changing environment it is unlikely that sufficient energy can be mustered to seriously question past commitments to national subsidiary autonomy.

### Power Base Difficulties

The power of the national subsidiary manager is based upon his control of the activities of the company in the host country. Coordination and integration of the activities of various functions and product lines within his domain are his key prerogatives and provide the base for his power. Rationalization, with its central management of investments, production scheduling and logistics, cuts at the heart of that power base. The manager's feeling of overall responsibility is threatened. A national subsidiary manager of a recently rationalized company once confided, "Now I am no more than a building superintendent." This is one of the central problems of rationalization: how to lead national or regional managers who were "kings in their fiefdoms" to relinquish their power for the good of the whole company.

National managers are likely to defend against rationalization by overplaying the importance of direct links with customers and the need to customize their products, in order to make rationalization seem undesirable. Corporate management is often ill-placed to assess the righteousness of their claims, particularly when government relations or employment issues are raised.

When these claims are well-founded, they may justify a partial rationalization only. Entire responsibility is left to the national subsidiaries for products that need local design and for which local production *does* matter to customers.[7] Sometimes corporate management may offer commitments to labor unions to not cut employment in the rationalization process, in order to gain their support and cut one possible objection by the subsidiary managers.

It is seldom possible to specify in great detail the exact benefits than can be brought by rationalization. The economies of production are not known in sufficient detail to make very precise cost projections. Some market share may be lost in one country, some gained in another, prices may be reduced, profits increased—but to assess precisely what the economic consequences of rationalization will be for each product in each country in terms of sales and contribution is next to impossible. Because of this fuzziness, national managers may slant a diagnosis or oppose necessary rationalization of part of their product line for fear of "what comes next."

These are the major problems that must be overcome in the diagnosis of a need for rationalization. They are not insurmountable but they must be carefully considered. Their existence explains why it is only in the face of the most pugnacious competition that rationalization is undertaken. It took intense Japanese and Eastern bloc competition to prompt European electrical motor and bearing manufacturers to rationalize their European manufacturing activities around common models. It is only when the need is blatant, and where sometimes the survival of the company (or one of its major subsidiaries) is at stake that rationalization is undertaken.

## Rationalization: Managing the Process

From the experiences of a few multinationals that were subjects of clinical research, some common characteristics and "do's" and "don'ts" emerge. The activities involved in a rationalization process fall into two broad stages: "start up" and reorganization of the production system. The rationalization process itself must, of necessity, span a period of several years, (a) because implementation needs to proceed in several steps and (b) because the physical tasks themselves take much time (relocation of production equipment, changes in production methods, closing of old lines, opening of new ones, training of workers and supervisors, etc.). Here I shall focus on the management process rather than on the physical process, and assume that the latter can be designed and carried out technically without major difficulties.

## Start Up

The diagnostic difficulties outlined above suggest the need to gain early commitment from subsidiary managers. A simple way to begin is to make an inventory of redundant product types. Such redundancies can be dramatically presented to national managers. For example, Philips' Radio, Gramophone and Television product group convened all its national subsidiary managers to show them hundreds of similar radio and television sets spread out on tables covering the ballroom of a large hotel, all made by one or another national subsidiary because it was "necessary for the market." In most cases the diagnosis can be expressed simply: the inventory shows obvious duplications and overlapping product ranges. SKF, the world's largest ball bearing manufacturer, with manufacturing operations in most European countries, concluded that the 50,000 different types of bearings produced in its five major national subsidiaries could easily be reduced to 20,000; a "core product line" of 7,000 types could be rationalized and made for inventory; and 13,000 other types could be made by one or another national subsidiary for domestic customers only.

Once the inventory of product types is completed, a business strategy analysis is undertaken to assess the special competencies of the various subsidiaries and to guide their specialization. This often is the first opportunity to consider the firm's business in a global perspective. Again, active cooperation with the national subsidiary managers is needed. To make the rationalization diagnosis part of an existing ongoing management process, where cooperation is already developed between subsidiaries, alleviates the fears of national managers and facilitates the evolution of their commitments. Often an established structure of technical coordination committees provides such an opportunity. Opportunities may also appear at times of broad strategic reassessment, when rationalization can be expected to draw upon the participating managers as a solution to overall strategic problems. Direct, active involvement of the management of national subsidiaries in the process is a prerequisite for the shifts in commitments required by a successful rationalization. Reliance on functional staff experts whose influence is based on recognized competence, rather than direct control or responsibility, to guide the diagnosis, first addressing the least controversial questions such as common nomenclature, product specifications, quality standards and manufacturing methods, helps to loosen former commitments and to start a cooperative process between subsidiaries. Similarly, first initiating rationalization of products identified as losers and of which no subsidiary is committed to production can provide a start for the process.

### Potential Pitfalls in Start-Up

At this early stage, there are several pitfalls to avoid. First, the development and acceptance of an overall blueprint is not as critical as the start of a cooperative process between subsidiaries and the affirmation that rationalization efforts are worth pursuing. These can be hampered by early formalization of the process or by the appointment of corporate coordinators or their equivalents who have undertaken exhaustive analytical studies to be used as blueprints. Powerful "coordinators" appearing as first signs of a strong central product management could stifle the process by taking it out of the hands of the national subsidiaries' managers, who would then resist it. The appointment of coordinators by the subsidiaries may also prove a hindrance: by creating a permanent but subordinate structure, the group of national subsidiaries may well prevent further implementation. A rationalization commitee chaired by a straw man and where real power would lie with subsidiary managers can easily lead to inaction because of haggling between subsidiaries or a consensus to do nothing. There is a difficult balance to be sought by top management: provide enough impetus to keep the process on its track; avoid pressure that may scare subsidiary managers.

Getting into complex and ill-defined products is another pitfall. Product design and manufacturing simplicity, well-defined customer groups and functions, low diversity within the product line, well-known distribution characteristics facilitate the emergence of a common appreciation of competition and make it more difficult for national managers to retrench behind technical and marketing differentiation arguments. In this sense it is much easier for a company such as SKF to reach a common rationalized "European" product line by 1981 than it is, say, for a Honeywell Information Systems.

A third potential pitfall to avoid is including too many subsidiaries in the process. Some countries discourage certain rationalization schemes for antitrust reasons (SKF left its U.S. subsidiary out of its rationalization plan), others are adamant in closing their borders to imports and promoting autarky (Philips left its Indian subsidiary out of its Radio plan), and others have many constraints and regulations that often discourage rationalization (e.g., Brazil, Mexico). Some of the autonomous subsidiaries are joint ventures, whose partners may be dismayed by rationalization and may strongly oppose it. Franko[8] found that the emergence of a regional structure in MNCs (which usually accompanies, with some lag, a rationalization process) was the single most important cause of joint venture problems in a rationalization. These problems should be closely studied before the attempt is made to bring a part-owned subsidiary into a rationalization plan. Finally, adding smaller subsidiaries to the scheme may well multiply administrative problems and diminish economic returns.

## Implementation of Changes in the Management Process _____

The very nature of the rationalization process is self-defeating: if left to the national managers, implementation may stop short of expectations as there is no overall institutionalized way of managing the rationalized system, and because national managers are not likely to relinquish power voluntarily once the sorest points have been dealt with.

At some point a centralized management body must be appointed, without, at the same time, reducing the strength of national subsidiary management. Most often the increasing sensitivity of host governments, and the internal trauma caused by sweeping reorganization, would rule out a complete sudden overall structural change which would suddenly replace national subsidiary preeminence with worldwide (or regional) management of all activities. Again, the problem to avoid is ruling by diktat and building an entirely new corporate architecture; one wishes instead to manage a smooth transition to a structure in which the central management body would acquire an increasing influence, but not absolute power.

The form taken by the new centralized management body may vary. In some cases it may be a new staff service, such as SKF's "General Forecasting and Supply System," based in the neutral ground of Brussels and organized to administer the rationalization. In other cases, such as the International Telecommunications Division of GTE, product vice presidents may be appointed at headquarters. In still other companies, the expansion of corporate headquarters or regional manufacturing staff may serve the same function. The form this reinforcement of central management takes will vary according to the idiosyncracies of each company and the products it manufactures.

Whatever its form, this new management is likely to be confronted with the same set of issues: how to gain influence over subsidiary activities without usurping the power of their managers in too brutal a fashion. Several problems of intersubsidiary coordination appear in the rationalization process; they cannot be easily solved by the subsidiaries independently, and so are likely to be brought to headquarters where top management can give them to the new product management unit to solve.

## Marketing Coordination

Once each subsidiary no longer manufactures a full product line, coordination of export marketing becomes important. Export orders have to be directed to the center and then allocated to the appropriate subsidiary. Beyond the mechanistic elements, there often remains a latitude of choice as to the source subsidiary, either because the order is not extremely specific or because several subsidiaries still manufacture comparable products. In some cases part of the rationalization design is to arrange for two or more sources so as to decrease vulnerability to strikes or other supply disruptions in any one of the subsidiaries. The ability to control allocation of export orders to the subsidiaries confers power over the subsidiaries to the central allocator.

The overall volume of activities of individual subsidiaries is also increasingly affected by export orders coming from the product management unit. Naturally, coordination of intersubsidiary shipments, production scheduling, and short-term logistics have to be managed jointly, particularly when the rationalization involves both segments of the product line and stages in the production process. The ability to expand or contract the volume of export business of particular subsidiaries, and thus affect their profitability, becomes a strong incentive for subsidiaries to fall in line.

Finally, both the global perspective of the product management unit and the lower costs yielded by rationalization may increase the worldwide overall market share of the company. Thus the slice of the cake offered to each subsidiary increases in size. In businesses where selling is an important, costly activity which requires much competence and intensive effort, a central unit is often better able to increase the overall return from the world market than a collection of autonomous subsidiaries competing against one another.

From the viewpoint of worldwide management, the maintenance of allocation flexibility in source and export markets constitutes a particularly powerful influence over the subsidiaries. For instance, the stable *a priori* allocation of geographic markets to certain subsidiaries in case of duplication effectively reduces the influence of product management. Similarly, the existence of only one source for one product effectively confers power on that source. So beyond the safety of supply questions, it is ironical to conclude that in order to be managed smoothly it may well be that rationalization has to remain incomplete!

## Production Programming Coordination

Usually concurrent with control over export marketing is the development of a central worldwide market analysis and forecasting system. The subsidiaries learn to depend on the central system for their own forecasting and planning as the share of exports (to other subsidiaries and possibly to third parties) in the sales of each subsidiary increases. Simultaneously, particularly when rationalization involves multistage production processes, production programs must be coordinated between the various subsidiaries—and the central management unit can become a broker and an arbitrator for the planning of intersubsidiary transactions.

## Technical Coordination

Regrouping the technical coordination structures with the new management unit may also provide the latter with a measure of control over the transfer of product and process technology between the subsidiaries. Linkages with the central research and development laboratories can also provide much influence. Controlling the transfer of new technology from the United States to European subsidiaries was a major source of influence of the product vice presidents at GTE.

## Investment and R&D Coordination

Control over capital and R&D expenditure can be delegated by top management to the worldwide product management unit. Because investments are now made with the aim of serving a worldwide market, individual national companies cannot be left in full control. Given their worldwide perspective combined with an in-depth knowledge of the business, product managers are best able to check, evaluate, and integrate into a coherent whole the investment proposals of the subsidiaries. This control was the single strongest source of influence for the corporate product directors at Dow Chemical.

## Difficulties and Pitfalls

The issues of export allocation, joint production programming, technical coordination, and capital and R&D fund appropriation have been found to provide a basis for establishing central coordination in order to complete the rationalization process. These issues enable the coordination center to assert influence over the subsidiaries and to foster integration and specialization of their activities. Yet there remain difficult questions which top management must consider with care.

First, timing rationalization with an overall business slump makes the rationalization process seem both more urgent and easier to implement. Brown Boveri's 1972 industrial motors rationalization plans were blasted by a mini capital boom in 1973 whereas SKF's managers attributed their own success in good part to the depressed markets of 1975–76. Taking advantage of new product introduction may also help cast the rationalization in a more positive light. It is also easier to plan for new machines and productions in a rationalized system than to start by relocating existing activities.

Second, sequencing is important. In a successful rationalization, behaviors and commitments change. Often the new patterns of interaction between subsidiaries induce shifts in power and status, causing great concern to managers. The various coordination issues are raised to bring cooperation between subsidiaries.

How and when to use these issues to gain influence upon subsidiaries most often rests with the decision-maker in the product management unit supported by top management. If he or she is too assertive, or a pawn of the coordination committee, the process is ruined.

Significant steps can best be taken when external sources of reward are present. At GTE, for instance, the worldwide product vice president obtained a huge telecommunication order which had to be allocated for capacity reasons; he used his power to allocate production as a means for gaining ascendancy and influence over national subsidiaries. Conversely, steps taken in direct conflict with outside events (as in the Brown Boveri case mentioned above) are likely to fail and jeopardize the whole process.

The sequence of moves to increase the influence of the worldwide product management unit(s) is subject to corporate veto control. Through their power over structure and their allocation of responsibility, top management can set the pace of the process and restrain overassertive managers. Beyond this broad conclusion, no general approach to the sequencing can be developed; sequencing depends on coalitions that can develop between subsidiary managers on the "feel" for the situation developed by the manager of the product coordination unit, and on the urgency imposed by competitive pressures.

Third, given his/her key role in managing the later parts of the rationalization process, a coordinator must be chosen carefully. There seem to be no general rules. Recognized substantive expertise and experience within the organization are important elements, but not sufficient ones. On the contrary, too much technical emphasis and task orientation would jeopardize the process. The most important element is the ability to provide energy, commitment and drive without using line authority. One means used by several companies is to appoint successful past subsidiary managers as worldwide product coordinators with the idea that they will know what is palatable to their former colleagues and what is not; their previous experience provides them with both an intellectual understanding and an emotional grasp of how to manage a subsidiary or an area. On the other hand, when one of the companies studied appointed *division* managers within its subsidiaries it reached out to recruit managers who had been running worldwide product groups for other MNCs. This company's top management hoped that some degree of reciprocal understanding between newly appointed subsidiary division managers and worldwide coordinators would facilitate a needed rationalization process in some of the activities they controlled. This quickly unlocked a tight situation and revitalized a rationalization that had been stalled for several years.

Wrong timing, sequencing and choice of coordinator(s) seem to be the most frequent cause of unsuccessful rationalization. They deserve much top management attention.

### Corporate Management Options to Support the Rationalization

Beyond direct management of rationalization, top management can facilitate its implementation and encourage central coordination in many ways. In particular, it is important to recognize that though national subsidiary managers have considerable autonomy prior to the rationalization, they do not operate in a vacuum: both the corporate and the host country environments contribute to shape the perceptions, premises, and commitments of managers. Therefore an important element of the rationalization process is to modify the organizational context within which subsidiary managers operate.[9] It is important to be aware of the set of administrative procedures that "shape the purposive manager's definition of business problems by directing, delimiting and coloring the focus and perception and determine the priorities which the various demands on him are given."[10]

Corporate management controls an array of variables which structure the context of subsidiary managers and can hinder or facilitate the rationalization process—in particular, the organization's architecture, the systems of measure, evaluation and reward and punishment, the flows of communication to and from subsidiaries, and the career paths of key managers.[11]

## Communication of Top Management Purpose ————————————————

It is important how the intent of rationalization and top management's commitment (or lack of commitment) to its success are signaled to national management groups. A mechanistic view of the social aspects of starting the process should be avoided. To increase the influence of product management without immediately decreasing the influence of national managers requires the development of a social interaction process. Top management's role in bringing product and host country preferences and their sponsors together is most important.

Series of worldwide planning meetings can be scheduled for a few days at a time, and what takes place outside the sessions is often as important as what takes place inside. Systematic patterns of communication between subsidiaries may be developed. Top managers should be personally involved in alleviating the fears of national managers and exploring their reservations. Only top managers and functional staffs constitute a relatively neutral source of arbitration for the conflicts that are bound to develop as rationalization is implemented. Because their actions are visible, top managers can also set precedents which signal the strategy they pursue and set the tone for relationships between host country and product managers.

## Changes in Measurement, Evaluation, and Reward Systems _____

Rationalization may not be compatible with tight national profit center accountability. Because decisions which affect the profitability of the subsidiaries are increasingly being influenced by worldwide product management units, maintaining tight profit center accountability leads to frustration and conflict. Thus, during the rationalization process a loosening up of the measurement, evaluation and control systems of national profit centers is needed. Similarly, an incentive system based on national subsidiary results may have to be replaced by one based on overall corporate or worldwide product group results. All companies stress the need for lenient measurement, evaluation and reward systems as a condition for learning and for disassociating personal financial risks from realignments in status and power.

## Career Paths and Management Development _____

It is important for top management to assess early in the rationalization process whether the role of subsidiary managers is likely to be diminished. If they have long represented the main level of general management, at some point during the rationalization process shifts in career paths should be considered. Though this is too broad a question to consider here, some of the key issues are worth mentioning. If marketing needs to be differentiated by countries and constitutes a critical task, splitting production and marketing could be considered: marketing would then be left to strong autonomous national companies headed by entrepreneurial managers. On the manufacturing side, only good plant managers are needed nationally. What scope remains for strong national managers? The development of international careers may be difficult, and national managers may resent being deprived of the perquisites of power and responsibility. Good national managing directors do not always make good international staff or product group managers. Also, for personal reasons country managers may loathe the expatriate status and relocations which accompany an international career path.

For all these reasons some attrition is unavoidable among national subsidiary managers and in some cases it may even be sought to facilitate the rationalization process. But the systematic replacement of strong national managers by mere caretakers is not advisable. With the growth of host governments' interventions, workers' participation, and the disillusionment with free trade and free investment, there is a need for the management of an integrated network to remain responsive to national conditions. We have also seen that the extent and benefits of a rationalization can hardly be clearly assessed in advance, and that not all productions, and not all countries can be rationalized without strong penalties. Therefore it is important to have a strong national management group sensitive to the needs of local interests as a balance to worldwide product managers who are likely to overlook national idiosyncracies.

## Conclusion

Rationalization is not only an economic and technical exercise, but also a complex social and organizational process which aims to develop an integrated multinational business capacity. Such a capability is particularly needed in developed countries and mature industries subject to intense price competition. It can bring economic advantages mainly through exploiting economies of scale.

Though an objective diagnosis of economic forces and of the benefits of rationalization is possible, it is likely to be hampered by difficulties of perception, commitment of managers, and power structure shifts. Start-up of a rationalization process requires new commitments from the national subsidiary managers and development of a central body that can draw influence from coordination of export marketing, worldwide market analysis, forecasting and production planning activities, improved export sales, changes in the production process, technology transfer and control over investments and R&D budgets. Full top management support must be provided to the coordinating body and to the rationalization efforts. Early pitfalls in the process include adoption of a firm "blueprint" without subsidiary managers' support, premature constitution of a coordination center, its dependence either on corporate or subsidiary management, attempts to rationalize complex products where the benefits of rationalization are not obvious, and inclusion of too many small or partly owned subsidiaries into the rationalization scheme. Later pitfalls may include poor timing, poor sequencing, lack of top management support and absence of administrative changes. Useful administrative changes include provision of a sense of purpose by top management, changes in the measurement, evaluation and rewards systems, changes in career paths, and staffing of key subsidiary positions.

Yet even carefully planned and well-managed rationalization processes may not be successful. Because rationalization challenges organizational commitments and power relationships and forces their realignment, many internal roadblocks have to be overcome to carry out the process. Some of these roadblocks are predictable in a planning stage, but overcoming them successfully requires constant top management attention at each stage in the process. The rationalization process deserves more research: I have merely tried here to suggest means of facilitating rationalization and some pitfalls to avoid when carrying out the process.

## Notes

1. Cited in Lawrence G. Franko, *The European Multinationals,* Stamford, Connecticut, Greylock, 1976.
2. William Abernathy, *The Productivity Dilemma* (forthcoming).
3. See, for instance, John S. McGee, "Economics of Size in Automobile Manufacture," in *The Journal of Law and Economics,* pp. 239–273.

4. See Boston Consulting Group, *Perspectives on Experience.* Boston, Massachusetts, 1968.

5. Richard G. Hamermesh. "Responding to Divisional Profit Crises." in *Harvard Business Review,* March–April 1977. Stuart Clarke Gilmore. "The Divestment Process," unpublished doctoral dissertation, Harvard Business School, Boston, 1975. Richard Normann, *Management and Statesmanship,* Scandinavian Institutes of Administrative Research, Stockholm, 1976.

6. Yves L. Doz, *Government Power and Multinational Strategic Management,* New York, Praeger (forthcoming 1979).

7. For instance, many prepared food products, and strategic products sold to governments or state-owned enterprises.

8. Lawrence G. Franko, *Joint Venture Survival in Multinational Corporations,* New York, Praeger, 1972.

9. Joseph L. Bower, *Managing the Resource Allocation Process,* Boston, Division of Research, Harvard Business School, 1970.

10. *Ibid,* p. 73.

11. See C. K. Prahalad, "Strategic Choices in Diversified MNCs," in *Harvard Business Review,* July–August 1976.

# II ———— STRATEGIES ————————————

# 3. RESTORING THE COMPETITIVE EDGE IN U.S. MANUFACTURING

## STEVEN C. WHEELWRIGHT

If one had surveyed U.S. practitioners and students of management in 1983 as to the competitiveness of U.S. manufacturing firms, there is little doubt that the majority would have responded that the United States was in serious trouble in several major industries. By mid-1984, with the economic recovery gaining steam, a similar survey would have found a much smaller group responding in like fashion, and most respondents would point to the increasing profitability of many companies—even in such industries as automotive products—as a sign of good health.

The speed with which perceptions change is just one of the challenges associated with addressing the topic of a competitive edge in a manufacturing-based enterprise. The purpose of this article is not to focus on whether or to what extent U.S. manufacturing has slipped in its worldwide competitiveness, but rather to describe what's possible (and required) if U.S. manufacturing firms are to secure a competitive edge in today's environment. However, as background and as a common reference point, it's useful to review briefly some of the available evidence and this author's conclusions from that evidence regarding U.S. manufacturing's current position.

- *U.S. manufacturing competitiveness has slipped in a broad range of industries.* One evidence of this is the list of industries compiled by Professor Robert Reich of Harvard University for a Senate subcommittee hearing in late 1980.[1] That list included sixteen industries—automobiles, cameras, stereo components, medical equipment, color television sets, power hand tools, radial tires, electric motors, food processors, microwave ovens, athletic equipment, computer chips, industrial robots, electron miscroscopes, machine tools, and optical equipment. In all these industries, according to Reich's research, the manufactured share of the worldwide output produced by U.S.-based companies fell by more than fifty percent between 1970 and the end of 1979. Clearly, the phenomenon of declining competitiveness is not limited to mature industries. A more thorough and updated analysis of U.S. manufacturing competitiveness and the forces impacting it is provided by Cohen, Teece, Tyson, and Zysman.[2]
- *The decline in U.S. manufacturing competitiveness has not been due primarily to labor costs.* The color TV industry presents an important counter to this

This article is adapted from a paper originally presented as part of the Transamerica Lecture Series, "Strategy and Organization for Industrial Innovation and Renewal," School of Business Administration, University of California, Berkeley, October 1, 1984. © 1985 by the Regents of the University of California, Reprinted/condensed from the *California Management Review* 27.3. By permission of the Regents.

common theme. As of 1984, there were five Japanese-owned color TV plants in the United States (two owned by Sony, one owned by Sanyo, and two owned by Matsushita). Although the number of imports is not insignificant, a majority of U.S. TV sales come out of U.S.-based plants, although a sizable portion of those plants are owned by Japanese firms.

■ *The relative competitiveness of U.S. manufacturing may be masked by cyclical swings, but those swings do not change the long-term prospects for such competitiveness.* For example, in the auto industry in the late 1970s and early 1980s, Detroit found itself in a disastrous situation—low volume, high breakevens, and high variable costs. Through dramatic efforts they were able to reduce their breakeven levels (but without much impact on variable costs), and with the economic upturn beginning in early 1983 and the mix shift back towards large cars, were able to reap tremendous profits, profits that were higher than those achieved in prior boom years. However, the basic facts with regard to cost per vehicle remained largely unchanged. For a small car, such as the Ford Escort, the U.S.-delivered (to the dealer) cost disadvantage when compared with their Japanese competitors was still $2,000 per car as of early 1983. Ford substantiated that through detailed cost analysis in their factories as well as in some of their Japanese joint-venture partners' and through a comparison of market prices where, in early 1983, the market price difference (lower in Japan) for the same car selling in Japan and the United States was almost $1,800. Economic upturns may make the company's bottom line look different, but they tend to have very limited impact on the long-term competitiveness of a given firm or country.[3]

The basic thesis of this article is that U.S. manufacturing is in competitive "hot water" in a broad range of industries, labor rates are not the primary cause of that, and a strengthening economy may temporarily mask the seriousness of the problem, but does not solve it. *The single most important explanation for the worldwide decline in U.S. manufacturing competitiveness is management's view of the manufacturing function, its role, and how that ought to be carried out. Thus, restoring that competitive edge requires a basic change in philosophy, perspective, and approach.*

This last point cannot be overstated. Widely held U.S. views of manufacturing are, quite simply, incorrect. At best, these hinder progress in manufacturing-based firms; at worst, they lead to continuing decline in worldwide competitiveness.

The balance of this article is divided into three major sections. The first describes the primary characteristics of the traditional U.S. view of the manufacturing function, outlines some of the reasons for its emergence, and illustrates several of the management actions that are a consequence of that behavior. The second describes a very different view of the manufacturing function—one that this author believes is a prerequisite to realizing manufacturing's competitive potential. The characteristics, underlying rationale, and resulting management behaviors associated with this contrasting view also are discussed. The third section uses three different types of evidence to support the position that a fundamental change in management's perspective holds substantial promise as a basis for restoring that competitive edge.

## The Traditional View of Manufacturing: Static Optimization ————————

The traditional U.S. perspective can best be described as *static optimization* of the manufacturing function. The essential characteristics of this philosophy of manufacturing, clearly evident in the area of *workforce management,* date from the turn of the century when Frederick Taylor and several of his colleagues initiated what was called "scientific management."[4] A basic tenet was that management should take more responsibility for how the worker performed the job, that hourly workers should be told what to do, and that their efforts should be controlled closely (often with incentive pay) to insure that they executed the orders given them. A good description of this view of workforce management is "command and control." (This description is very similar to that of military science of that same period, where to command and control were added the terms communication and intelligence. Communication referred to the transmittal of data—from manager to worker—and intelligence referred to collecting the data needed to monitor the worker's effort.)

Taylor's description of Schmidt, an hourly worker engaged in loading a rail car with pig iron, is a classic illustration of command and control. Through systematic data gathering and analysis of Schmidt's activities, Taylor determined the "best" way for him to perform his job. The set of steps comprised by the "best" way was then conveyed to other workers and through close supervisory control, incentive pay, and evaluation, average productivity for the workforce was raised substantially. Although the adoption of such methods is disjointed, almost autonomous departments did improve productivity significantly, the carryover effect on management's views of manufacturing was substantial and not altogether desirable.

Basically, management came to view the workforce as a source of energy where eight hours work for eight hours pay was the goal. In addition, since white collar workers and staff were "smarter" (better educated and higher paid) than hourly workers, it followed that decisions should be made at higher levels in the organization, and less discretion left to the shop floor. This increased need for coordination and systems foreshadowed most of today's manufacturing information systems, which in the United States are driven largely by coordination requirements. (For example, material requirements planning systems are aimed at conveying to the shop floor the exact set of actions to be taken, when, and for what products and materials.)

What resulted is management's view that it should be able to plan and decide the best course of action in advance. Implementing this plan is simply a matter of getting the workforce and the first-line supervisors to execute it. This view of workforce management adheres to the oft-quoted phrase, "If it ain't broken, don't fix it." That is, the way to keep things running smoothly in the factory is to stabilize what goes on there, rather than to continually change (and improve) what goes on. Since management is in control of decision making and information dissemination, it is in a position to directly affect such stabilization.

Unfortunately some major negatives emerge from this approach to workforce management. These include a decline in workers' motivation and interest in their work, a decline in suggestions for improvement coming up from the bottom of the organization, the disassociation of workers from overall firm objectives and goals (since it's not their responsibility), and the gradual split into an us versus them (worker versus management) mentality. Much of today's U.S. labor relations environment is a reflection of this static optimization of the workforce and its role.

Perhaps as a means to accomplish the desired stability in the workplace or simply as a consequence of narrowing the scope of the worker's responsibility, management's perspective on *technology* took on the characteristics of static optimization. This has become particularly apparent in such fundamental aspects of technology as the relationship between product development and manufacturing process development, the role of process improvement (internal to the organization versus external), and the benefits anticipated from more automated production processes.

The static optimization view of manufacturing leads most organizations to view product development as the creative task and manufacturing startup as the execution task. Thus, new products are developed in sequential fashion with R&D taking full responsibility initially and then tossing that responsibility to manufacturing at a later stage. This connection is often described as the "over the wall" transition. R&D does whatever it wants and then throws the design "over the wall" to manufacturing. With little or no interface between the two functions, manufacturing must figure out on its own what to do with the product designs it receives.

The development of new production technologies is considered of secondary importance. Thus, process evolution in many firms and industries is viewed as an afterthought, lacking the competitive significance of product developments. (It's interesting to note that in petrochemicals and a handful of other process-intensive industries, this view has never held sway.) Processes are developed, not in anticipation of new product opportunities, but only as required by the pricing realities of the marketplace (costs must be lowered) or the product characteristics as defined by R&D (the existing process can't be used to make the new product). Because little advance thought has been given to process evolution, manufacturing naturally turns to the apparent "experts" on such process developments—the equipment suppliers. Thus, the expertise for process technology resides largely outside the organization, and the majority of that expertise must be captured by buying the equipment produced by those suppliers. (The point here is not that equipment is purchased from a third party, but that the purchaser sees little need or value in developing technical expertise in the manufacturing processes represented by that equipment.)

Furthermore, this view of process technology asserts that automation is justified primarily as a means of reducing costs. That is, volumes must grow to the point where automation can be justified on a cost improvement basis before it will be considered. Most firms that hold this view make certain that any automation they adopt does not alter the product or its performance in the marketplace. Simply stated, the automated process has to do exactly what the older, less automated process has been doing but at a lower cost. This is the traditional view of substituting capital for labor.

One result of this view of technology and its role in the manufacturing firm is that the anticipated product development and new product performance plans are seldom accomplished. Chart 1 summarizes for one firm its expected (before-the-fact) resource allocation and production cost curve and contrasts them with its actual

## Chart 1
### RESULTS OF TRADITIONAL PRODUCT DEVELOPMENT/MANUFACTURING STARTUP

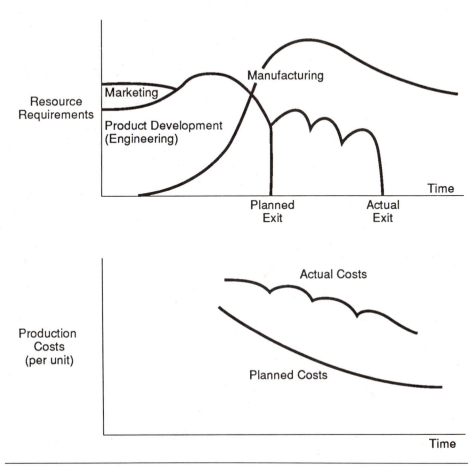

*Source:* In-company study.

experience on the basis of an examination of its recently introduced products. The results are striking. Product development's anticipated withdrawal from a new product project never takes place because the design as handed to manufacturing is not fully producible. Subsequently, a series of major redesign efforts are undertaken. While each of these redesigns improves the product, each redesign results in higher costs. Two or three additional redesigns often take place before the product is abandoned and the next generation product is introduced.

In firms with a static optimization view of technology, manufacturing processes lag significantly behind what is possible (i.e., their process technologies tend to be old and outdated), and they have much difficulty bringing new equipment onstream, complaining continually that the supplier didn't tell them enough about what was required to operate it. They find that they've bought equipment from a supplier with no concern for the organizational capabilities required to take advantage of it. Furthermore, since automation is not allowed to affect the product as it is received by the customer, only the most obvious manufacturing technology projects are pursued. Usually, those become ad hoc forays into more advanced manufacturing technologies, rather than a systematic development, evolution, and building of the organization's skills at the most desirable technologies.

This view of manufacturing is largely a *hierarchical or vertical* view which continually subdivides and specializes the function. As a result, it is difficult for the organization to handle tasks that require integration skills, especially if integration is required across functions at multiple levels of the organization. When such coordination is needed, information must flow up to a fairly high level in manufacturing before it can be transmitted either to R&D or marketing. Consequently, many small, but cumulatively significant, improvement opportunities that might be identified in operations simply aren't worth the effort to pursue. Additionally, when new tasks of an opportunistic nature that require an integrated response arise, they're likely to be ignored or given secondary emphasis by the organization since they require capabilities (integration and coordination) that are not readily available.

Overall, the static optimization view keeps manufacturing primarily in a responsive mode with little opportunity to carry out long-term systematic developments. Thus, while significant effort may still be expended to deliver today's products as well as tomorrow's, the performance never quite measures up to the expectations and manufacturing never becomes a source of competitive advantage recognizable to customers. That may still result in very satisfactory performance, especially when that firm's competitors have a similar perspective on the manufacturing function. However, if such competitors replace this traditional view with a more progressive view that's better suited to today's environment, those adhering to the traditional one will eventually find themselves at a competitive disadvantage.

## The Progressive View of Manufacturing: Dynamic Evolution _____

A much more progressive view is one that can best be described as *dynamic evolution.* In many respects this philosophy is the antithesis of the static optimization view. The dynamic evolution view holds that the problem of production will never be solved. Rather, it is necessary, possible, and desirable to continually improve the function and its contribution to the overall business. This improvement comes not simply from better execution but from ongoing, fundamental change in what is done and how that is carried out.

To contrast this view with the static optimization view, it is useful to look first at the area of workforce management. Unlike the view of Frederick Taylor, which was one of command and control of *effort,* this view entails investing in the problem-solving skills of the workforce and then focusing their *attention on those problems that they are in the best position to solve.* This might be described appropriately as knowledge management.

*To operationalize this view in an organization, workers' problem-solving skills must be developed and the needed information provided so that they can determine what the problems are and how they ought to be solved. Thus, the concern is not for getting eight hours' work for eight hours' pay, but getting the workers' best efforts (both mental and physical) applied to the areas about which they know the most and have the most influence—generally their immediate working area and their production tasks. As described by a colleague, the concern is shifted from* reluctant conformance *under static optimization to* motivated performance *under dynamic evolution. This, of course, requires a very different kind of information system, one that is real-time and problem-identifying/problem-solving oriented.*

Another characteristic of this view is that since workers have major inputs as to how their work can best be carried out, it's no longer appropriate for supervisors to exercise first-order control—telling them what to do and then measuring to see if they've done it. Rather, second- and third-order control are required, the former consisting of systems and procedures and the latter consisting of shared goals and objectives. The production environment is considered much more worker-dependent than that of the static optimization view, and one that involves much more delegation of responsibility, all the way down to the shop floor.

Incentives also must be realigned to reward workers for improvements, to insure that new learning is captured by the organization, and to make continual improvement, rather than fits and starts, the result. A widely publicized mechanism for carrying out this philosophy of workforce management is quality circles. As practiced by Japanese firms, quality circles are simply a tool that incorporates this perspective on the workforce role into the manufacturing function. Quality circles are not an organizational behavior ploy, nor are they strictly a quality enhancement ploy or a way to keep the workers happy, as they might be if used in a static optimization manufacturing environment. Rather, quality circles are the vehicle for focusing, developing, and applying worker problem-solving skills.

This dynamic evolutionary view of the workforce and its contribution has important implications for middle management. Their task is no longer the secure one of having all the answers and telling those lower in the organization exactly what should be done. It is much more one of facilitating a team approach, where problem-solving responsibility is shared with workers. For many middle managers accustomed to the static optimization view of the world, this can be a very threatening change in their environment. Similarly, in a unionized plant, such a change has major implications for the union and its role. One thing that can be extremely helpful when a union moves to support the dynamic, evolutionary view of the workforce is for the union to play a major role in developing the technical competence and problem-solving skills of the workforce.

Upon reflection, most union leaders as well as managers agree that the best way to raise wages is to raise the skills and value added of the workforce. In turn, the best way to increase such skills is through ongoing training and development. It follows naturally in the dynamic, evolutionary view of manufacturing that ongoing training of lifetime employees should be the norm, not the exception. Increasing technical competence then serves as a major basis for worker problem solving, and as a way for management to continually upgrade the contribution of individual workers and work groups.

The characteristics of the dynamic, evolutionary view also can be seen clearly in the area of technology. New product development, which was a sequential procedure under static optimization, becomes truly a team sport. It involves a group of peers who work as equals across functions throughout the duration of the product development/manufacturing start-up activities.

Complementing this view of product development and product technology is the view that process technology is not made up of production equipment alone; it comprises the systems, the people, the equipment, and all aspects of an organization's productive capabilities. Consequently, process technology is viewed as proprietary to the organization even though some elements are acquired from outside suppliers and other organizations. Thus process technology becomes something to be planned for systematically, in parallel with product development activity. The goal of such process development is to provide the capabilities that the product technology will need to support and enhance the latter's translation into distinctive products and customer services.

With product and process technology elements more fully integrated and coordinated, two other aspects of technology management come into sharper focus. One is the fact that over time, and in the majority of cases, significant improvements in technology result from a long series of incremental, usually small, steps and not from a few big breakthroughs. This reinforces the importance of in-house technical capabilities as the key to continued improvement. The other is that shorter development cycles can be achieved, providing three specific types of benefits. The first is better timing of new product and new process introduction. Through product and process coordination such timing can be tailored to the market and competitive realities, and better timing leads to shorter development cycles and thereby more flexibility either to introduce sooner or to start later making it possible to incorporate more recent technical developments.

A second benefit of shorter development cycles is improved quality, not only of the product produced (because the designs tend to be more manufacturable and tend to be better suited to the processes available), but also of the basic designs (they are more functional and provide better features). This design quality comes from better focus, better learning, and more responsiveness to the information generated during the product development steps. Basically, with shorter cycle times, those involved in technology development activities can do a better job of capturing the learning that is going on and there is less forgetting than there is with longer cycle times.

The third benefit associated with shorter development cycles is reduced cost. Reductions in per-unit production costs result from faster more trouble-free manufacturing start-ups, more producible designs, and more flexibility where needed. Costs of the design process also are lowered, since fewer steps need to be repeated, overhead on the project is lower when its duration is shortened, and people's time and effort tend to be focused more effectively.

A major plus for the dynamic, evolutionary approach is that, with the emphasis on manufacturing process evolution, automation is viewed primarily as a source of product enhancement rather than simply cost reduction. That is, advanced manufacturing processes are considered a way to produce better products, products that could not be manufactured by others who lack such automation and ongoing process improvements.

The dynamic evolutionary view of manufacturing has other important characteristics with far-reaching competitive implications. One is that as an organization develops this perspective, it significantly enhances its ability to handle what might be referred to as "horizontal" tasks. These tasks cut across functions in the organization at multiple levels. Unlike vertical tasks that can be divided up and handled by increasing levels of specialization, horizontal tasks are considerably more complex and not easily subdivided. A number of tasks facing manufacturing firms in today's environment tend to be of such a horizontal nature. New product development/manufacturing start-up is clearly such a task. Also, the topics of quality and productivity are both of this nature in that they involve multiple functions working at multiple levels to make significant improvements.

Finally, organizations that adopt the dynamic evolution view tend to keep all of their functional areas—marketing, control, manufacturing, and R&D—in much better balance, each making significant contributions to the firm's competitive advantage. Instead of one function (generally either marketing or R&D) calling the primary shots and taking a dominant role in developing the competitive advantage for the entire business, all functions work as a team to develop that competitive advantage. In such firms strong arguments can be made that each of the functions makes a significant difference to the firm's success in the marketplace. The result is an organization that can use its resources more efficiently and that can better combine and integrate their contribution than would be the case where one or more functions is treated as having a "static optimization" role.

## Contrasting the Impact of Static Optimization and Dynamic Evolution _____

There are significant advantages to pursuing the dynamic evolution view in place of the more traditional static optimization view of manufacturing. While additional direct evidence contrasting these two philosophies and their impact on performance clearly is needed, limited data from three related aspects do lend support to this conclusion. These three areas are those of historical analogy, the experience of a handful of companies that have shifted from one view to the other, and U.S. experiences with the adoption of new manufacturing processes.

From a historical perspective, recent works by Alfred Chandler, Nathan Rosenberg, and Wickham Skinner indicate that the British and American experiences with industrial development during the late 1800s can be characterized as the British following the static optimization philosophy and the Americans following the dynamic evolution philosophy.[5]

Because of their history and the maturation of their manufacturing firms, the reaction of the British to many of the developments and innovations of the late 1800s was to use them in firms that were narrowly focused, depended on external organizations for technological applications, and had a history of workforce-management confrontation. American firms, on the other hand, tended to integrate technology much better within the individual firm, to address both the worker and management aspects of new technical requirements, and to develop systematically both processes and products that would meet new emerging needs. Chandler summarizes some of these differences by contrasting the British and American approaches to technology.

*They [the British] failed, not in research, but in development. They failed because they did not create the critical organizational linkages. They failed to build the organization, hire the personnel, and set up the facilities so central to the development of new processes and products. They failed to carry out the developmental processes that are so much more costly in manpower and money than basic research. In particular, they failed to forge the linkages between research, design, production, and marketing so critical to rapid and effective development of new proudcts.*[6]

Rosenberg adds to this description of the American approach the fact that, within companies, within industries, and at a national level, the Americans tended systematically to measure and seek to understand the processes that were emerging.[7] Such measurement became the basis of application for those processes and their continued improvement and refinement. Skinner adds that, because of the pervasiveness of these evolving technologies, it was critical that managers possess the technical competence to interact with those processes and become designers of their productive capabilities, rather than simply caretakers of existing manufacturing assets.[8] Skinner describes such people as Andrew Carnegie (in the steel industry) as veritable architects and creators of new opportunities using these evolving process and product capabilities, whereas the British tended to view managers as the owners' agents and thus caretakers of what already existed.

More recent evidence of the differences in impact of these two philosophies can be seen by examining two organizations—General Electric Dishwashers and Mitsubishi Automotive Australia—that have sought to move from the static optimization view of manufacturing to a dynamic evolution view. The first example is the dishwasher unit of General Electric's Major Appliance Business Group.[9] In the late 1970s this business unit, located in Louisville, Kentucky, at GE's Appliance Park, had a twenty-year-old cost-reduced product design, production processes that were ten to twenty years old, a strong union environment of the traditional U.S. adversarial type, and a workforce with average seniority of 15+ years. However, because of GE's many strengths, this division also had the number one position in the U.S. market for dishwashers, with approximately a third of the market.

It was at this point that the division proposed to senior management that it be given $18 million of capital to make the next iteration of improvements in the product. Management's response was that if such an investment did nothing to significantly enhance GE's position, perhaps the money would be better spent elsewhere. Division management responded with a serious look at their environment to determine what would be required to significantly enhance General Electric's position. The result was a revised proposal for senior management consideration that included a major overhaul of how the workforce was used in the division, a major new product design, and a new approach to both product and process technology that would upgrade them in an interactive and evolutionary fashion.

This proposal, which has an eventual price tag of $38 million, represented a shift from a static optimization view of manufacturing to a dynamic, evolutionary one. Included in the details of the proposal were changes in the work environment, the skills and participation of the workforce, and management's communication and commitment to them. Also included were a complete redesign of the product with a change from a steel tub and door to a plastic tub and door and an order-of-magnitude improvement in the quality levels (both in the plant and from suppliers). Finally, the production processes were to be significantly altered to incorporate automation that would complement the new product design and deliver the desired quality levels.

This much more aggressive approach was approved by senior management and a three-year effort was launched to change the division's view of its manufacturing function. Within the first nine months of product introduction in 1983, this new dishwasher was a solid success on several performance dimensions, as summarized in Table 1. Continued improvement was budgeted (and achieved) for 1984. Additionally, the organization made substantial progress in operationalizing the new view of manufacturing.

The second example comes from the automotive industry in Australia. In the late 1970s, when the Chrysler Corporation found itself in increasing difficulty, it chose to sell many of its "losing" operations. One of those was its auto assembly operation in Adelaide, Australia. That plant had been run under the static optimization philosophy for decades and recently had suffered major losses. Mitsubishi Corp. of Japan acquired the plant from Chrysler and made several significant changes in manufacturing's role and management's view of it, moving it toward a dynamic evolution view. Some of those changes included developing new information systems (that were problem-solving oriented), eliminating a number of layers in the organization so that managers and workers could interact more closely and more effectively, adopting new management values with regard to worker and manager roles, and implementing a just-in-time manufacturing system which put the emphasis on continued incremental improvement on the factory floor. The results of this approach, contrasted with the last year in which Chrysler owned 100 percent of the plant, are shown in Table 2. By 1981, not only had the plant become the most profitable in the Australian auto industry, but its market share had improved significantly (from

### Table 1
### GE DISHWASHER—RESULTS

| Performance Measure | 1980/81 (Actual) | 1983 (Actual) | 1984 (Estimates) |
|---|---|---|---|
| Service Call Rate (Index) | 100 | 70 | 65 |
| Unit Cost Reduction (Index) | 100 | 90 | 88 |
| Number of Times Handled (Tub/Door) | 27/27 | 1/3 | 1/3 |
| Inventory Turns | 13 | 17 | 28 |
| Reject rates (Mech./Elec. Test) | 10% | 3% | 2.5% |
| Productivity (Labor/Unit Index) | 100 | 133 | 142 |
| Other: 70% fewer part numbers, 20 pounds lighter, worker attitudes (positive $2\times$, negative $0.5\times$) | | | |

*Source:* Published GE data, see Robert H. Hayes and Steven C. Wheelwright, *Restoring Our Competitive Edge—Competing Through Manufacturing* (New York, NY: John Wiley & Sons, 1984).

### Table 2
### MITSUBISHI AUTOMOTIVE—AUSTRALIA

| Performance Measure | 1977<br>(Chrysler-Owned) | 1981<br>(Mitsubishi-Owned) |
|---|---|---|
| Profitability | ($27.8M) | $17.7M |
| Productivity (Index) | 100 | 215 |
| Assembly Hours/Car | 59 | 24 |
| Market Share (Overall) | 9.4% | 13.3% |
| Market Share (Mid-sized) | 4.0% | 34.4% |

*Source:* McKinsey & Company study, Sydney, Australia (1982)

9.5 percent to 13.3 percent) and the market share of its primary targeted segment (the mid-sized automobile) improved from 4 percent to 34.4 percent!

A third type of evidence of the impact of these two philosophies comes from recent experiences of U.S. manufacturing firms in dealing with "new" manufacturing technologies. Perhaps one of the most highly touted technologies on the manufacturing front today is CAD/CAM (computer-aided design/computer-aided manufacturing). While everybody's talking about it and some firms are adopting it, the results from the use of CAD/CAM are clearly mixed and slow in coming. In one of the most thorough studies of the early 1980s as to the effectiveness of CAD/CAM and what influenced that effectiveness, McKinsey and Company identified every U.S. user of this new technology and analyzed their approach to the technology and the results achieved.[10] One of the most significant conclusions of their study is summarized in Chart 2. They found that adopters of CAD/CAM could be placed into one of three categories:

- those who used it simply as a productivity tool for existing individual workers (designers and engineers);
- those who used it within a single department (most often the product development group); and
- those who used it across multiple functions and at multiple levels.

The overall effectiveness and impact of these three groups of adopters differed significantly, as did the time it took to begin to realize results. As shown in Chart 2, those using the technology as a simple substitute for existing processes found real productivity benefits, but largely of a cost-reduction nature. Basically, a very powerful tool was being used primarily as an electronic pencil. In the second category were adopters who were making major changes in a single department and the way in which that department approached its tasks, but not in the way that department interacted with other parts of the organization. These firms not only obtained cost-reduction benefits (as expected when substituting newer and better technology for an older one) but also enhanced product features because the new technology provided designers with capabilities not previously available to them. In the third category were those who took a total business perspective on the new technology who pursued

## Chart 2
### APPROACHES AND RESULTS OF CAD/CAM APPLICATION

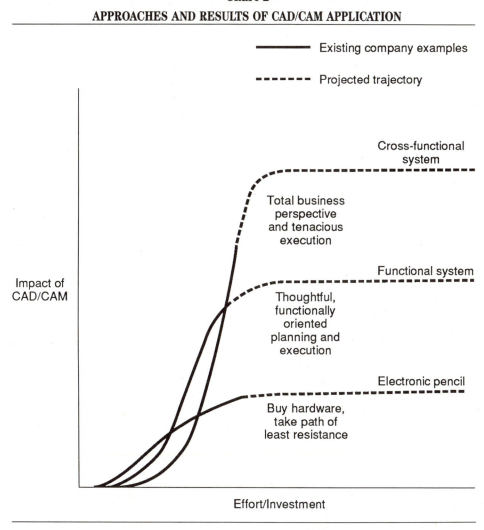

*Source:* McKinsey & Company, 1984.

its capabilities across functions and throughout several parts of the organization. For these firms, the technology became a competitive opportunity significantly enhancing the quality of their designs and shortening the product development cycle time. McKinsey found that horizontal integration across tasks at multiple levels was the key difference that distinguished this third group from the first two. Thus, although the first two gained significant benefits, they realized only a fraction of the full competitive potential.

A second technology that has appeared on the manufacturing scene in recent years is that of just-in-time production. The basic notion, as originally developed by Toyota, is "elimination of waste." (Such waste covers all activities that do not add value directly for the customer-extra operations, overproduction, defective products, and earlier than necessary operations.) Operationally, substantial emphasis is placed on reducing production cycle times by eliminating work-in-process inventories and shortening equipment set-up times. When combined with a problem-solving role for the workforce and an information system that focuses attention on problems, substantial benefits can be achieved. However, U.S. experiences in adopting just-in-time methods suggest that they consist not simply of a handful of techniques for addressing such tasks as work-in-process reduction and set-up time reduction, but represent an entire philosophy of ongoing improvement in manufacturing. For most U.S. organizations, such a view requires a shift in philosophy from static optimization to long-term, ongoing, dynamic improvement.

## Concluding Comments _____

Having read this author's assessment of two very different perspectives on manufacturing and the consequences of each, one might well raise the question of why U.S. management hasn't seen these differences, and responded quickly and broadly to adopt the dynamic evolution view. At least three points appear to be relevant. Those points elucidate why such a shift is necessary yet difficult, and thus provide a useful summary of this entire discussion.

First, when the static optimization view emerged in the early 1900s, it provided substantial benefits to U.S. manufacturing. It recognized the characteristics of the environment at that time—in terms of education level, the shift from loosely affiliated craft groups to large factories, rapidly expanding demand, and opportunities to make order-of-magnitude improvements by adopting and mastering recently developed manufacturing technologies. Because of its success, there was little pressure to adopt a different approach, and management's focus (and resources) were gradually directed to more pressing areas.

Second, because pressures for a change in that manufacturing view developed gradually and in various forms—none of which "obviously" required such a fundamental change—management could look for other easier, near-term fixes, with some immediate benefits. Thus changes in world-wide competition, domestic market growth rates, the nature of U.S. labor relations, etc. didn't fully combine to significantly heighten pressures on U.S. manufacturing until the 1970s. If anything, the stability of the 1960s and U.S. predominance on the world economic scene caused U.S. management to become overconfident, perhaps even "soft," and miss many of the early warning signals of the need for change.

Third, the shift from the static optimization to the dynamic evolution view of manufacturing is a pervasive and fundamental one. It is not a matter of simply changing a few *decisions* or even making one major issue or *event* the focal point for change. Rather, it requires a change in the *process* of management, encompassing a broad range of behaviors, practices, and decisions as well as philosophies and values. Fundamental change such as this can be accomplished only over years of sustained effort.

The difficulty of making such a change is both the challenge and the opportunity. While making that change increases the commitment, effort, and resources required to be successful, once mastered, it becomes a significant strength, an ongoing basis for competitive advantage. Because it is so difficult to imitate and fits with the environment manufacturing firms are likely to continue to face for the coming decade, it's the best type of competitive edge.

## References

1. Robert B. Reich, *The Next American Frontier* (New York, NY: Times Books, 1983).
2. Stephen Cohen, David J. Teece, Laura Tyson, and John Zysman, "Competitiveness," Center for Research in Business, University of California-Berkeley, IB-1, November 1984.
3. William J. Abernathy, Kim B. Clark, and Alan M. Kantrow, *Industrial Renaissance* (New York, NY: Basic Books, 1983).
4. Frederick W. Taylor, *The Principles of Scientific Management* (New York, NY: Harper & Bros, 1947).
5. Alfred D. Chandler, Jr., "From Industrial Laboratories to Departments of Research and Development," in Robert H. Hayes and Kim B. Clark, eds., *Adversaries in Alliance: Managing the Productivity-Technology Dilemma* (Boston, MA: Harvard Business School Press, 1985); Nathan Rosenberg, "The Commercial Exploitation of Science by American Industry," in Hayes and Clark, eds., *Adversaries in Alliance;* Wickham Skinner, "The Taming of Lions: How Manufacturing Leadership Evolved 1780–1984," in Hayes and Clark, eds., *Adversaries in Alliance.*
6. Chandler, op. cit.
7. Rosenberg, op. cit.
8. Skinner, op. cit.
9. For a more complete description of this situation, see Robert H. Hayes and Steven C. Wheelwright, *Restoring Our Competitive Edge—Competing Through Manufacturing* (New York, NY: John Wiley & Sons, 1984).
10. McKinsey & Co., *Restoring Manufacturing Entrepreneurship* (Cleveland, OH: McKinsey & Co., 1984).

# 4. EVOLVING GLOBAL MANUFACTURING STRATEGIES: PROJECTIONS INTO THE 1990S

KASRA FERDOWS, JEFFREY G. MILLER,
JINICHIRO NAKANE, AND THOMAS E.
VOLLMANN

Our surveys of nearly 1,500 large manufacturers in Western Europe, North America and Japan during the last three years indicate intriguing similarities and differences in the manufacturing strategies of the companies in these regions. Around the world, manufacturers are placing an overwhelming emphasis on new products, quality and the use of computer power in manufacturing. But, while doing so, most European manufacturers appear to be engaged in a re-examination of some of the structural elements of their manufacturing systems, the Americans to be experimenting with a broad range of new ideas—among which their focus on fundamental approaches to quality control and sophisticated computer-based information systems stand out, and the Japanese to be mobilising for the development of unique production processes and technologies.

Drawing upon the data collected through these surveys, in this paper we first describe the differences that we observe in the pattern of strategic directions and priorities for the manufacturers in each region. Second, we discuss how the companies in each region are implementing their manufacturing strategies. Third, we discuss the vulnerable elements in the pattern of dominant manufacturing strategies which we observe in each region. Finally, we speculate on the nature of manufacturing capabilities which are likely to emerge in each region into the 1990s, and the particular problems that may develop as a result.

## Projections into the 1990s

Our analysis of evolving manufacturing strategies is based on the data we have collected through our Global Manufacturing Futures Survey from 1983 to 1985, from 1,500 manufacturers in Western Europe, North America and Japan, and is presented in four parts: first, we describe the differences that we observe in the pattern of strategic directions and priorities for the manufacturers in each region. Second, we discuss how the companies in each region are implementing their manufacturing strategies. Third, we discuss the vulnerable elements in the pattern of dominant manufacturing strategies which we observe in each region. Finally, we speculate on

Kasra Ferdows, Jeffrey G. Miller, Jinichiro Nakane, and Thomas E. Vollmann, "Evolving Global Manufacturing Strategies: Projections into the 1990's," *International Journal of Operations and Production Management* 6.4 (1985) 5–14. Reprinted by permission.

the nature of manufacturing capabilities which are likely to emerge in each region into the 1990s, and the particular problems that may develop as a result.

The similarities and differences that emerged were intriguing, the differences, however, outweigh the similarities. Some of these differences, especially with respect to the Japanese, are in the strategic orientations of the business units with respect to manufacturing. There are greater differences in the way companies from different parts of the globe seek to attain their strategic objectives in manufacturing. These differences in action plans can be explained by fundamental differences in viewpoint, local concerns and problems, culture and history.

In broad and relative terms, most European manufacturers appear to be preoccupied with re-examination of some of the structural elements of their manufacturing systems. The Americans are experimenting with a very broad range of new ideas, but seem to be focusing on fundamental approaches to quality control and sophisticated computer-based information systems. The Japanese are focused on the development of unique production processes and technologies.

## The Global Manufacturing Futures Survey _____

The data for this research has been collected through our Manufacturing Futures Survey of 1983, 1984 and 1985. These are annual surveys of large manufactures in Western Europe[1], Japan[2], and North America[3] which we have conducted with the help of colleagues in our respective universities: Boston University originated the American Manufacturing Futures Survey in 1982; INSEAD and Waseda University started the European Manufacturing Futures and the Japanese Manufacturing Futures Surveys in 1983.

The survey consists of a rather detailed questionnaire which is mailed to about 1,000 of the largest manufacturers in each region every year. The questionnaires are addressed to a senior manufacturing manager in the company and mostly answered by them. The response rate in different regions and different years have varied between 10 per cent and 25 per cent. Table 1 shows the number of respondents by year in each region. The respondents were from a large variety of industries which were fairly evenly distributed among the machinery, electronics, consumer packaged products, industrial products, and basic industries.

The object of this effort is to build an international data base on how manufacturing is managed in large companies:

- the strategic directions and competitive priorities these manufacturers are setting for themselves;
- their current concerns;
- what they are doing or planning to do to improve their manufacturing capabilities.

The data base (which to our best knowledge is unique) allows intra-regional trend analysis, industry-specific analysis, and empirical tests of a variety of general research hypotheses relating to manufacturing management. Our purpose in this report is to present an inter-regional comparison. The data base is particularly suitable for this purpose because most questions in the three regional surveys are identical.

## Table 1
### NUMBER OF RESPONDING BUSINESS UNITS BY YEAR

| Region | 1983 | 1984 | 1985 |
|--------|------|------|------|
| Europe | 150 | 154 | 168 |
| North America | 209 | 213 | 174 |
| Japan | 260 | 197 | 186 |

## Competitive Priorities

The primary function of a manufacturing strategy, as suggested by Hayes and Wheel-wright[4], is to guide the business in putting together the manufacturing capabilities that will enable it to pursue its chosen competitive strategy over the long term. Examining the competitive priorities which manufacturers are setting for themselves, therefore, provides a clue for understanding the pattern of manufacturing capabilities that are being developed. These competitive priorities—or, using Skinner's term, 'manufacturing missions'[5]—are what the company strategy demands from manufacturing.

Table 2 shows the rank ordering of these priorities in each of the three regions studied. The Japanese differ most in their priorities from the Europeans and Americans. Consistently, in the last three years, they have emphasized the ability to offer low prices and the capability to deal with rapid design changes. The Europeans and the Americans, however, in remarkable agreement, have been placing high priority on their abilities to offer high quality products and to make dependable delivery promises. Quality also scores high with the Japanese, but not as high as it does with the Americans and Europeans.

The convergence of answers within each of the three regions, and especially in Japan, is rather remarkable: almost every Japanese manufacturer in our sample considered the ability to offer low prices to be highly important for competing successfully in the next five years; only about three out of five European and North American manufacturers in our sample did so. (Note that in post-survey interviews most Japanese manufacturers said that they did, indeed, weigh most highly the *ability* to offer low prices, but that they would prefer to have low costs consistent with this emphasis, and the highest prices possible. In other words, their real priority was in low cost production, not necessarily low selling prices.) Four out of five Japanese manufacturers considered the ability to make rapid design changes to be highly important; again only about three out of five Europeans and Americans did so. On the other hand, almost every American manufacturer and nine out of ten European manufacturers considered the ability to offer consistent quality to be of the highest importance competitively; seven out of ten Japanese agreed. And slightly more than eight out of ten Americans and Europeans considered the ability to make dependable delivery promises to be highly important; less than seven out of ten Japanese did so.

## Table 2
## COMPETITIVE PRIORITIES (1983 AND 1984 SURVEYS)

| Europe | North America | Japan |
|---|---|---|
| Consistent Quality (1,1) | Consistent Quality (1,1) | Low Prices (1,1) |
| High Performance Products (3,2) | Dependable Deliveries (3,3) | Rapid Design Changes (2,2) |
| Dependable Deliveries (2,3) | High Performance Products (2,2) | Consistent Quality (3,3) |
| Low Prices (4,4) | Fast Deliveries (4,4) | High Performance Products (4,4) |
| Fast Deliveries (6,6) | Low Prices (6,5) | Dependable Deliveries (5,5) |
| Rapid Design Changes (5,5) | After-Sales Service (5,7) | Rapid Volume Changes (6,6) |
| After-Sales Service (8,8) | Rapid Design Changes (7,5) | Fast Deliveries (8,7) |
| Rapid Volume Changes (7,7) | Rapid Volume Changes (8,8) | After-Sales Service (7,8) |

The numbers in parentheses are the rank in the 1983 Survey and in the 1984 Survey.

The overall picture which emerges is that the Europeans and Americans seem to be striving for higher quality, while the Japanese are primarily seeking lower costs and flexibility. One interpretation of this picture is that the Americans and the Europeans are aiming at overcoming what they perceive to be the relative deficiencies of their manufacturing compared to the Japanese, whereas the Japanese, having been relatively successful in both quality and delivery management, are now aiming at developing a new competitive edge which combines flexibility with low cost manufacture. We think this is a reasonable interpretation as it fits the other signals (described later in this paper) which we discern from our data. This interpretation raises the prospect of North American and European firms finally meeting the Japanese threat in terms of quality and delivery, at some time in the future, only to then find a new 'lowcost-flexible manufacturing' threat before them.

The strategic manufacturing priorities of these producers must be interpreted in terms of their overall strategic directions. Table 3 depicts these directions in terms of eight characteristics in rank order of their importance as indicated by survey respondents. Four of these characteristics relate to product-market relationships. Of these four, there is no statistically significant difference between the manufacturers in the three regions. As we said before, the strategic directions of these firms are much the same. They aim foremost at increasing their shares in existing markets with new products.

But, with respect to three of the remaining characteristics, the Japanese seem again to stand apart from the Americans and the Europeans. The Japanese are emphasising backward integration more than their European and American counterparts, and are relying less on quantum changes in their business, through either acquisitions or divestitures. More upstream integration normally increases the role of the manufacturing function in the competitive strategy of the company. Less emphasis on divestiture and acquisition can be interpreted as greater commitment to existing businesses. Together they indicate a pattern which is in agreement with the proposition that the Japanese, more than the Americans or the Europeans, focus

## Table 3
## STRATEGIC DIRECTIONS (1983 SURVEY)

| Europe | North America | Japan |
|---|---|---|
| New Products/Existing Markets (4.2) | New Products/Existing Markets (4.0) | New Products/Existing Markets (4.3) |
| Market Share/Existing Markets (4.0) | Market Share/Existing Markets (3.8) | Market Share/Existing Markets (4.1) |
| New Markets/Existing Products (3.7) | New Products/New Markets (3.4) | New Products/New Markets (3.9) |
| New Products/New Markets (3.5) | New Markets/Existing Products (3.3) | New Markets/Existing Products (3.2) |
| Growth by Acquisition (2.8) | Growth by Acquisition (2.5) | Backward Integration (3.0) |
| Withdrawing from Business (2.5) | Withdrawing from Business (2.4) | Forward Integration (2.3) |
| Forward Integration (2.2) | Forward Integration (2.4) | Growth by Acquisition (1.4) |
| Backward Integration (2.1) | Backward Integration (2.1) | Withdrawing from Business (1.2) |

The numbers in parentheses are the average weights on a scale of 1—5, where 1 is no emphasis and 5 is critical emphasis over the next five years.

This table shows the 1983 responses; the responses in 1984 were almost identical to 1983.

on the enhancement of existing capabilities to develop competitive advantage. This is in agreement with the views of most other observers of Japan, such as Moritani[6], Hayes[7] and Schonberger[8].

## Implementing Strategies

How are these strategic directions and competitive priorities translated into specific programmes and action plans in manufacturing? Examination of the concerns of the senior manufacturing managers responding to the survey provides a first clue. In our survey we gave each respondent a choice of up to 34 different items related to various aspects of manufacturing management, and asked them to indicate the extent to which they were concerned about each item. The respondents could add more. Table 4 shows, for each region, a list of the top thirteen items (in rank order) which have been rated to be of most concern. (From a strictly statistical point of view, these rankings should be regarded as approximate to generally ± one position, i.e., non-contiguous rank differences are generally statistically significant.)

Consistently over the last three years all three regions expressed highest concern over producing to high quality standards. The message from the competitive priorities—which, as mentioned above, indicated a high emphasis on competing on the basis of quality—has clearly been received by manufacturing. The Japanese, again very consistently in the last three years, follow this with an almost equally high

## Table 4
## CONCERNS: 13 HIGHEST RATED AMONG 32 CHOICES (1983, 1984 AND 1985 SURVEYS)

| Europe | North America | Japan |
|---|---|---|
| 1. Manufacturing to Quality Standards (1,2) | Manufacturing to Quality Standards (1,1) | Manufacturing to Quality Standards (1,1) |
| 2. Overhead Costs (2,1) | Overhead Costs (3,2) | Yield, Rejects (2,2) |
| 3. Material Costs (4,4) | New Product Introduction (2,4) | New Product Introduction (4,4) |
| 4. New Product Introduction (5,5) | Sales Forecasts (7,8) | Process Technology (5,5) |
| 5. Sales Forecasts (7,6) | Yield, Rejects (5,10) | Qualified Supervisors Available (3,3) |
| 6. Indirect Labour Productivity (3,3) | Vendor Quality (*,*) | Aging Workforce (11,10) |
| 7. Inventories (9,9) | Production Lead Times (*,*) | Too Many Engineering Changes (*,*) |
| 8. Delivery on Time (10,15) | Indirect Labour Productivity (4,5) | Product Line Breadth (*,*) |
| 9. Production Lead Times (13,14) | Inventories (*,6) | Delivery on Time (8,7) |
| 10. Yield, Rejects (11,17) | Material Costs (6,7) | Direct Labour Productivity (7,8) |
| 11. Aging Plant and Equipment (14,12) | Delivery on Time (*,*) | Indirect Labour Productivity (9,12) |
| 12. Qualified Supervisors Available (8,11) | Process Technology (9,12) | Overhead Costs (*,8) |
| 13. Government Regulations (15,10) | Vendor Lead Times (*,*) | Inventories (*,*) |

Ranking in the 1984 and 1983 surveys in parentheses; in general, there are statistically significant differences between non-contiguous ranks. (*) Prior rank less than (10).

---

concern over improvement in yield and reduction of rejects. The Americans seem to have started to pay more attention to the yield and reject problems (moving from the tenth place in their 1983 list of concerns to about the fifth place in 1985). But concern over yield and rejects is not in the forefront of attention of most European manufacturing managers (although it has moved up from the seventeenth place in 1983 to about the tenth place in 1985).

The Europeans and Americans, on the other hand seem more concerned with costs and productivity: high or rising overhead and material costs, as well as low direct and indirect labour productivity, are higher on their lists of concerns than for the Japanese. It appears that Americans and Europeans are at least as concerned about costs as they are about quality. They are also more concerned with the accuracy of sales forecasts (an item which is remarkably low in the Japanese list).

Another similarity among the three regions is in their concern with introducing new products on schedule. The manufacturers in all three regions indicate that the average life cycle for their products is decreasing, and that they (and particularly the Japanese) expect their products to be more customised in the next five years. It is, therefore, reasonable to see the regions being highly concerned with introduction of new products on schedule.

A major concern in Japan is with falling behind in process technology. Many of the Japanese companies in our survey are generally regarded as technological leaders in their fields, yet consistently we find the typical Japanese manufacturing manager being highly concerned about this issue. We find this significant and we shall return to it later. The Japanese are also concerned about the availability of qualified supervisors—a concern somewhat shared by the Europeans but not as much by the Americans.

The overall picture which emerges shows considerable similarities in the concerns of the manufacturing managers in the three regions. However, there are also telling differences among the three regions. Telling, that is, because they are indicative of motivation for action on various issues. If we only look at the differences, we find the American and the European manufacturing managers relatively more concerned with cost related issues, and the Japanese managers relatively more occupied with quality at several levels. This picture raises a question about the consistency between the concerns of the Americans, the Europeans and the Japanese manufacturing managers, and their competitive priorities. Are the relatively high concern over costs expressed by the Americans and Europeans justified when as a competitive priority the ability to offer low prices is below a number of other factors? Conversely, if the Japanese are putting the ability to offer low prices high on their list of competitive priorities, why do they seem to be relatively less concerned with the cost related issues?

Our data provide no direct answers to these questions. Our interpretation of the data, backed up by interviews with a number of managers, is that in America and Europe, almost regardless of the competitive priorities set for the company, the manufacturing managers continue to be under direct and short-term pressure to perform well on costs. The Japanese, on the other hand, seem to consider that costs will be reduced in the long term if they concentrate on quality improvement, process technology, and finding qualified supervisors and workers to run their operations. This interpretation suggests that the time frames and indeed the basic paradigms for strategic planning and action in Japan and in the West are substantially different.

The way these strategies are being implemented in different parts of the world becomes clearer when we examine the specific actions of manufacturers over the last several years. In our survey we asked for information on the specific improvement efforts, relating to the management of manufacturing, that had been undertaken in the company. Table 5 shows the programmes most frequently undertaken by manufacturers in each region over this period.

Again there are many similarities among the three regions. Many manufacturers in each region have been working on their production and inventory control systems, on programmes for motivating the direct labour force, on supervisory training, and

**Table 5**

## TEN MOST IMPORTANT ACTION PLANS (1983, 1984 AND 1985 SURVEYS)

| Europe | North America | Japan |
|---|---|---|
| Direct Labour Motivation (2,1) | Direct Labour Motivation (4,5) | Flexible Manufacturing Systems (6,3) |
| Production and Inventory Control System (5,*) | Developing New Processes for New Products (6,1) | Automating Jobs (1,2) |
| Automating Jobs (1, ) | Vendor Quality (*,*) | Developing New Processes for New Products (5,6) |
| Integrating Manufacturing Information Systems (7,4) | Production and Inventory Control Systems (1,2) | Production and Inventory Control Systems (2,1) |
| Vendor Quality (*,*) | Statistical Process Control (*,*) | Quality Circles (4,4) |
| Supervisor Training (6,3) | Integrating Manufacturing Information Systems (3,3) | Integrating Manufacturing Information Systems (*,10) |
| Integrating Information Systems Across Functions (*,5) | Zero Defects (*,*) | Vendor Quality (*,*) |
| Developing New Process for New Products (3,2) | Developing a Manufacturing Strategy (*,*) | Worker Safety (*,*) |
| Reducing the size of the Workforce (*,*) | Integrating Information Systems Across Functions (10,9) | Value Analysis (9,*) |
| Manufacturing Reorganisation (*,10) | Statistical Product Quality Control (*,*) | Reducing Lead Time (*,7) |

Ranking in the 1984 and 1983 Surveys in parentheses; in general there are statistically significant differences between non-contiguous ranks. (*) Prior rank less than (10).

on integration of information systems, within the manufacturing function. But examination of the differences is also revealing.

The Japanese manufacturers continue to put efforts into quality circles; Americans and Europeans did the same for a while in 1984 but reduced their efforts in 1985. The Japanese clearly are putting an increased emphasis on flexible automation and new production processes. They show a more aggressive profile than the Americans and Europeans for nearly every one of the process technology-oriented action plans covered by the survey (only the top ten items are shown here; the rest included computer-aided design, computer-aided manufacture, investment in process engineering, etc.). It appears that they are banking on the promise of these new technologies to provide the capability to deliver low costs with a high degree of flexibility, which are the foremost priorities of the Japanese.

The Americans, and to a large extent the Europeans, also seem to be converging on new technologies at a fast pace, but in different ways. The Americans, for example, seem to be framing most of their programmes for technological improvement in terms of information systems (software) rather than in terms of process technologies such as flexible manufacturing systems (FMS), and robots (hardware), like the

Japanese. This is seen by the high frequency with which American (and European) firms are working on integrating information systems both within manufacturing and across functional boundaries.

The Americans have recently been emphasising a variety of programmes for improving quality. Vendor quality, zero defects, and statistical quality control programmes were perceived to be much more important in 1985 than in prior years. This change represents a shift to programmes which are much more consistent with competitive priorities.

In 1984, two-thirds of European and American and half of the Japanese manufacturers reduced the size of their workforce. Substantially fewer in all three regions did so in 1985. The Europeans, in particular, seem to have replaced the reduction of the workforce with programmes for motivation of the workforce. This suggests fewer lay-offs and more attention being paid to the remaining work force.

Further insights into the action plans of manufacturers are provided by examination of the list of future programmes which managers in each part of the world feel are *most important* (as opposed to most used). In Japan, flexible manufacturing systems have consistently been identified as being most important by over 13 per cent of the sample. No surprise here. In the United States, statistical quality control, developing new processes for new products and a host of information system projects are identified as being most important. Again, we see the emphasis on quality and software. In Europe, the most important activities have been developing a new manufacturing strategy, work on improving labour/management relationships and reorganising the manufacturing function. This suggests that European manufacturers are in the midst of restructuring their manufacturing to a far greater extent than their American and Japanese counterparts.

## Dominant Manufacturing Strategies

To get an overall idea of how the manufacturers in these three regions are acting out their manufacturing strategies one needs to put together all that we have gleaned from the data on concerns, priorities and plans. Any attempt at encapsulating these findings in one or two short sentences carries the risk of oversimplification or, worse, superficiality. Nevertheless, to make our points in the rest of this paper clearer, we take this risk.

Our overall interpretation is that a large number of Japanese manufacturers are banking on aggressive deployment of technology to achieve economic flexibility in manufacturing. They seem to be focused as a group on developing 'breakthrough' capabilities that fundamentally change the way manufacturing is done. They appear to be developing flexible process technologies which will yield both low costs and flexibility. This technological thrust appears to focus on process development as viewed more from the perspective of the manufacturing engineer than from the viewpoint of the computer scientist. Their highest ranked projects for the future are framed in terms of physical process models such as FMS, rather than in terms of information flows. These efforts seem to be entirely consistent with their competitive priorities, their major concerns and their culture.

The European and American manufacturers' competitive priorities appear to be focused on doing the fundamental things better, especially with respect to the quality and dependability of their processes and deliveries. Overall, costs appear to be viewed as a major problem area rather than as the centrepiece of a fundamental long-range competitive strategy. This puts these firms in the position of trying simultaneously to do everything well within the context of their existing operations. We see both the Americans and the Europeans planning on broad portfolios of the future actions, ranging from technological development to improving their human capital. In contrast to the Japanese, the technological thrust of these firms seems to spring more from the framework of the information systems specialist than from that of the process engineer. Between the North Americans and the Europeans, the major difference appears to be in the extent to which their planned activities focus on quality and information technologies as opposed to activities which develop their people and organisations. The Americans are much more heavily focused on the former, and the Europeans on the latter.

## Conclusions and Speculations on Future Manufacturing Capabilities _____

It has been proposed by one of the authors of this paper that the Japanese companies aim essentially at a predetermined sequence of priorities in manufacturing:

1. first high quality must be produced;
2. *then* delivery reliability must be achieved;
3. *then* production costs must be lowered;
4. finally production flexibility must increase.

Our data support this proposition. The Japanese manufacturers in our sample seem to have passed the quality and delivery reliability stage, and now are focusing on costs and flexibility.

Achievement of manufacturing flexibility, however, may require a different set of resources and capabilities from those which helped the Japanese attain their preeminence in quality. To develop unique capabilities in flexible manufacture, as the Japanese aim to do, they must develop a good part of the needed manufacturing technology in-house. They are already doing that. Our data show that for their production process technology, the Japanese tend to look much more internally (i.e., inside the company) than externally. American and European firms are more likely to look to outside suppliers for their technologies.

But what if the technological problems that they have to solve turn out to be knotty and intractable, and entangle their companies in difficult situations? Their drive for quality, for example, was to a large extent based on worker-initiated, careful, meticulous and continuous improvement in the management of production. The drive to flexible manufacturing, on the other hand, seems to require greater reliance on technical and scientific resources aimed at making quantum breakthroughs. The new focus on the latter may lead them to dismantle those dedicated work teams and efficient social structures that provide the basis for their steady, small, incremental improvements in quality. For them, manufacturing management in the 1990s may be focused on delicately balancing the need for change with the need to preserve existing capabilities and strengths.

The similarity in the responses of the various Japanese manufacturers to the survey (and in subsequent interviews) must be noted here. In contrast to the rich diversity of strategies and action plans in North America and Europe, the similarity in the approaches of the Japanese firms in our sample is striking. There is some risk in their, as a country, putting all their eggs in one basket. It is, however, difficult for us to assess this risk against the benefits of having a clear and uniform focus.

If the Japanese are successful in their attempts at a breakthrough, they will aggravate the vulnerability of the dominant manufacturing strategy of the Americans. With their focus on sophisticated information systems, despite their already acknowledged abilities in these areas, the Americans run the risk of overlooking simplification of the production process itself. The competitive value of a complex system for the management of manufacturing evaporates as the production process is simplified beyond a certain point. Changing the production process in the direction of 'repetitive manufacturing' (even with no change in aggregate output) may be more effective than designing sophisticated information systems for managing a 'job shop'. In short, *because* of their ability to design and operate complex systems, and *because* of their openness to new ideas and fast adoption of them, the Americans run the risk of leaving their manufacturing processes in a more complicated state than they need to be, or, in fact, of increasing rather than decreasing the level of complexity in them.

A second area of vulnerability for the typical North American manufacturer is suggested by the conflicting goals they seem to be trying to achieve. The North Americans' chief concerns seem to be focused on cost, while their strategic priorities and much of their current activities focus on quality. It is difficult to conceive of cost oriented actions which will improve quality (although the converse is not difficult to understand). The Japanese goals on the other hand, as mentioned before, are clearer and more consistent: they reduce costs by focusing on quality first. Recently, more American manufacturers seem to have accepted this new paradigm and have started to act upon it. We expect this trend will continue in the next few years, and that we will be witnessing more achievements from American manufacturers along the quality dimension. We expect that one of the continuing challenges for Americans into the 1990s will be the development of new performance measurement and accounting systems which will help them to resolve the conflicts between a purely financial orientation and other dimensions of competitiveness, such as quality.

The problem for the European manufacturers is of a different nature. The European emphasis on people and organisation calls for change: change in the size of organisations, workforce, technology, and other parameters of manufacture. These are rather drastic changes. It seems that the European manufacturers are discarding some of their traditional competitive strategies and are embarking on new ones. Given the common perception of the widening technological and industrial gap between Europe and the other two world industrial powers—Japan and the United States—there may not be many other options.

The issue, then, for many European manufacturers is how quickly they can achieve these structural changes. How long will it take to choose and implement a new strategic course for the company, to set clear objectives for manufacturing in light of the new strategy, and to marshall all the resources which would be required to develop specific manufacturing capabilities? Would the time required exclude the European manufacturers from becoming major global competitors in certain fast-moving industries?

The European manufacturers are probably burdened with more external obstacles in their efforts to move fast in their intended directions. Varied but entrenched cultural values, deep industrial traditions, complex industrial relations and other geopolitical factors have so far tended to hinder change. But there are also rich scientific and technical traditions in many European countries. The task—and preoccupation—of the European manufacturers would be to chart a swift course among these complex forces as they implement their strategies into the 1990s.

One area of vulnerability facing the Japanese and the North Americans and Europeans is the shortage of people with the skills required to move to new technologies. Today's 'smart' technologies requires a combination of the skills of the process engineer and the MIS specialist. How far can the Japanese progress with the best process engineers but with limited MIS skills? How far can the best MIS specialist in Europe or North America advance without understanding process design? What kind of manager is needed to manage operations based on such different capabilities? These questions will face everyone as they move to the 1990s.

# References _____

1. Ferdows, K. and De Meyer, A., "Manufacturing Futures Survey, Europe," *Operations Management Review,* Winter 1985.
2. Nakane, J., "The 1985 Manufacturing Futures Project: Summary Data of Japan," Waseda University Systems Science Institute, 1985.
3. Miller, J. G. and Vollmann, T. E., "Manufacturing Futures Survey: North America," *Operations Management Review,* Winter, 1985.
4. Hayes, R. and Wheelwright, S., *Restoring Our Competitive Edge,* John Wiley & Sons, New York, 1984.
5. Skinner and Wickham, "Manufacturing—Missing Link in Corporate Strategy," *Harvard Business Review,* May-June, 1969.
6. Moritani, N., *Japanese Technology,* Simul Press, Tokyo, 1982.
7. Hayes, R., "Why Japanese Factories Work," *Harvard Business Review,* July, 1981.
8. Schonberger, R., *Japanese Manufacturing Technique,* Free Press, New York, 1982.

# 5. TECHNOLOGY ACQUISITION: LICENSE AGREEMENT OR JOINT VENTURE

## PETER KILLING

*J. Peter Killing is an Associate Professor at The University of Western Ontario's School of Business Administration, London, Canada.*

Funding for this research was provided by the Fund for Excellence, The University of Western Ontario, The Department of Industry Trade and Commerce (licensing study) and the Foreign Investment Review Agency (joint venture study).

This paper suggests the conditions under which firms wishing to acquire technology should use each of two types of license agreements and two types of joint ventures. An examination of 74 license agreements and 30 joint ventures shows when firms do use each of the four types, and allows some interesting observations on the market for technology.

The market for technology appears to be small, inconsistent and fragmented. A firm might be offered the same technology in a simple license agreement from one supplier, while a second demands a 50-50 joint venture. Many technology suppliers will not enter joint ventures in which they own less than 50 percent, creating a very thin market for joint ventures in which the technology dependent firm is a majority owner. The implications of these factors, and the way in which technology prices appear to be established, are discussed. The paper is unusual in that it looks at the market from the viewpoint of the buyer of technology, rather than the seller.

It was in approximately 1920 that a Swedish chemical firm decided that it would stop doing its own research and development work and would instead concentrate on searching out the leading chemical process technologies in the world and acquire them under license, or if the firm with the technology insisted, through the use of joint ventures. In 1974, this company, which had by that time become the largest chemical group in the country, was delighted to learn that its 14 year old 50 percent owned polyethylene joint venture was recorded to be the most profitable firm (on a percentage basis) in Sweden. The general manager of the venture indicated recently that in the opinion of all concerned, the company's strategy of acquiring outside technology has been a marked success and will continue.

This successful Swedish venture raises a number of questions for managers of any nationality. Most simply put the issue is, "Why go it alone if you can get the help you need on reasonable terms?" Managers who buy technology suggest quietly that it is often an underpriced commodity, especially when one considers that the package of information received may include marketing assistance, as well as product

Peter Killing, "Technology Acquisition: License Agreement or Joint Venture," *Columbia Journal of World Business* 15.3 (Fall 1980): 38–46. Reprinted by permission.

design and production process specifications. It is, they argue, very much less expensive to purchase such information than to learn from one's own mistakes. However, absorbing knowledge from others is not quite so simple as it sounds, the Swedes notwithstanding, and establishing and maintaining a working relationship with a firm which is technically superior to your own requires some specialized attention and skills.

This paper is unusual in that it addresses the subjects of licensing and the formation of joint ventures from the point of view of the technologically dependent firm. Much more common are studies of the options open to firms which have technology, such as exporting, foreign direct investment, joint venture, and license agreement. This paper considers the conditions under which a firm without technology should try to acquire it, via each of two types of license agreement and two types of joint venture. Examination of data on 74 license agreements and 28 joint ventures lead to the observation that the market for technology is fragmented and inconsistent, and the implications of this fact for technology-hungry firms are discussed.[1]

## A Prescriptive Model _____

The first portion of this paper describes a normative model, which suggests the conditions under which technology deficient firms should and should not make use of current technology license agreements; current and future technology license agreements; joint ventures in which they own a strong controlling interest; and joint ventures in which they are approximately or exactly equal owners with the technology supplier. This model is based on a fundamental proposition, which is as follows:

> *The more the technology dependent firm needs to learn about the business to which the technology in question relates, the stronger the relationship it needs to form between its personnel and those of the technology supplier.*

It is easy enough to transfer hardware-blueprints, specifications, price lists, product samples; but much harder to ensure the transmission of the intangible "knowhow" which is in the minds of those who use the hardware. Effective transfer of knowhow requires a strong personal relationship between sender and receiver, and it is to this fact that the proposition relates. Once the sender begins to know the person to whom he is transferring information, he can tailor his messages very specifically taking into account the other's knowledge and skills. Conversely, the recipient of the information, as he gets to know the sender better, can realistically assess the information being supplied. If the sender indicates, for instance, that an engineering development is likely to take six months, the recipient can assess this, with experience, as to its likely degree of optimism or pessimism.

The strength of the relationship between sender and receiver will be a function of the amount of contact between personnel of the two firms, and the degree of commitment on the part of the technology supplying firm to ensure that real learning takes place. Both of these factors—contact time between the firms and level of supplier commitment—will be a function of the type of license agreement or joint venture chosen. Since gaining the commitment of the technology supplier and access to its personnel generally cost money, in one form or another, one does not want to overdo it. The objective is to match the strength of the linkage with the task at hand.

The need for learning on the part of the dependent firm will depend on the extent to which it is moving away from its established base of knowledge and skills. The further it moves away, the more learning is required. If the major areas of learning in relation to a new product are technical and marketing, and in each of these the skill needed for the product can be identical to existing skills, related to existing skills, or unrelated to existing skills; then the following chart of diversification possibilities can be created.

As the diagram suggests, several of these nine categories will be combined to create four strategies of diversification for subsequent analysis. *Unrelated* diversification means that in neither area is the skill need for the new product related to skills existing in the firm. *Loosely related* diversification is a label used to indicate the situation in which either the marketing or the technical skills needed are unrelated to those existing in the firm, but not both. When either or both needed skills are related to those in the firm (and neither is unrelated) the strategy will be one of *closely related* diversification. The final category, *existing business,* is used to denote the situation in which both the needed technical and marketing skills already exist in the firm.

The arguments developed thus far are summarized as follows.

**Figure 1**

**RELATIONSHIP BETWEEN EXISTING SKILLS AND THOSE REQUIRED FOR THE NEW PRODUCT**

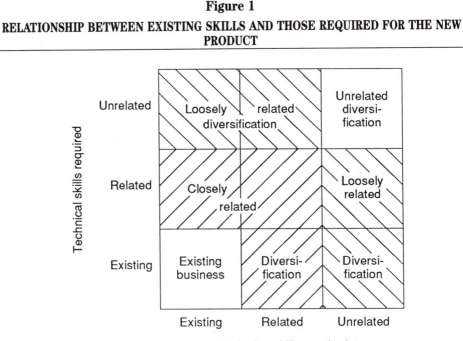

This logic flow will be used to postulate the correct use of two types of license agreements and two types of joint ventures. Before doing so, each of these four agreements will be discussed and the differences between them explained. The license agreements are the *current technology* agreement, which gives the licensee access only to technology which is in existence at the time the license agreement is signed, and *the current and future technology* agreement, which states that new development work done by the licensor in a specified product area during the life of the agreement, as well as current technology, will be transferred to the licensee. It is apparent that the current and future technology agreement offers a much greater opportunity for contact between licensor and licensee, as meetings between personnel from each firm may take place for a number of years, in comparison with the one time contact of the current technology agreement. A 1975 study of license agreements by this author revealed an average yearly contact time between licensor and licensee, in current and future technology agreements, of 45 employee days, with a range from 0 to 275.[2] In a current technology license agreement, whatever contact there is between firms—the exact amount will depend upon the complexity of the technology—will all take place in the first year of the agreement. In such an

**Figure 2**

**LOGIC FLOW**

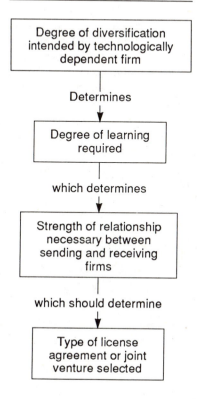

agreement, the licensor will not assign personnel to the licensee to assist with information transfer, and this happens very seldom even in current and future technology agreements. Licensees have been known, however, to assist the information flow in current and future technology agreements by permanently assigning someone to the licensor's plant.

The two types of joint venture examined in this study are the *majority joint venture,* in which the technology dependent firm owns 70 percent or more of the voting stock, and the *50-55 percent joint venture* in which the technology dependent firm owns 50 to 55 percent of the joint company. Generally speaking, there is greater motivation and opportunity for contact between firms in joint ventures than exists in license agreements. A 1977 study,[3] examining the use of license agreements and joint ventures by British firms in India, presented data to support this statement. Howard Davies found that 78 percent of the joint venture made use of personnel from the technology supplying parent to supervise plant construction, versus 26 percent for license agreements. In 28 percent of the joint ventures, managers from the technology supplier joined the venture, whereas this was true for only 55 of the licensees. Transfers of plant level personnel occurred in 48 percent of the joint ventures, versus 15 percent of the license agreements. Somewhat more detailed data were collected by this author from a sample of 30 joint ventures involving Canadian, American, and Western European firms. Differentiation was made between majority joint ventures and 50–55 percent joint ventures and a distinction was drawn between employees permanently assigned to the venture by the technology parent, and those on short term visit, longer loan, and permanent assignment. In contrast to the figures shown below, it should be noted that in only one of the 74 Canadian and British license agreements which will be referred to subsequently was an employee permanently assigned to the licensee by the licensor.

The probability of employees being assigned to a joint venture in which the technology supplying parent has 45 to 50 percent of the equity is clearly greater than in those cases in which it has 30 percent or less. These are generally production managers and or engineering managers. The only surprise in Figure 4 is the fact that there were as many as four ventures (16 percent in the category) in which technology parents owned 45–50 percent of the venture and did not lend or assign personnel to the venture. However, two of these ventures were so small that they had no permanent employees, and were using part time help from the local parent.

### Figure 3
### PERSONNEL TRANSFERS

| | Employees From Technology Parent | | | |
| --- | --- | --- | --- | --- |
| | Visits only | On loan | Permanently assigned | Total |
| Majority joint venture | 1 | 2 | 2 | 5 |
| 50-55% joint venture | 4 | 4 | 17 | 25 |
| Total | 5 | 6 | 19 | 30 |

**Figure 4**

**EXPORT RESTRICTIONS AND PRODUCT AGE**

| | Allowed To Export* | | Product Age** (years) | | |
|---|---|---|---|---|---|
| | Yes | No | 0—3 | 4—10 | 10+ |
| Current technology | 18 | 6 | 20 | 4 | 3 |
| Current and future technology | 6 | 26 | 5 | 14 | 20 |
| | 24 | 32 | 25 | 18 | 23 |

*The export statistics relate only to products manufactured by Canadian licensees. It is illegal for a licensor to restrict a British licensee from exporting within the EEC.

**Product age is the time in years between a product's first world introduction and its introduction by the licensee.

*Source:* P. Killing, Manufacturing Under License, *Business Quarterly* (Winter 1977).

A third was performing extremely poorly, and the Canadian manager attributed this poor performance directly to the fact that the foreign parent had not lent them any technical help for the first few years.

The linkage between the last two steps of Figure 2 should now be clear. If a weak relationship with a technology supplier is all that a firm requires, it should try for a current technology license agreement. As the strength of the required relationship increases, the target should be a current and future technology license agreement, or a majority joint venture, and in cases where the strongest link is needed, a 50–55 percent joint venture. The reason for not using a stronger link than strictly necessary is that the cost of the agreement to the technology dependent firm generally goes up as the strength of the linkage increases. This cost may be reflected in other ways than royalty rates. For instance, current and future technology license agreements generally have a much higher incidence of export restrictions than do current technology agreements. They are also more readily available on older products. The data below are from the 1975 licensing study.

The cost difference between a current and future technology agreement and a majority joint venture is less clear cut. In fact, the president of one Canadian firm using a majority joint venture argued that on a cash flow basis, a majority joint venture could be less expensive than a current and future technology agreement. He reasoned that in giving a technology supplier 20 percent of the equity of the new venture in exchange for its technology, the cash (dividend payments) going to that parent would only be about .5 percent of sales. He based this calculation on after tax earnings of approximately 5 percent of sales, and a 50 percent dividend payout ratio. This fee is not only far lower than that of most license fees, but it is also payable at the discretion of the licensee, and can be withheld until the venture is stable and profitable. The factor not accounted for is, of course, that the technology supplier owns 20 percent of the joint company, and this will eventually be a cost to the Canadian manager.

The high cost which managers attribute to the 50–55 percent joint venture is not strictly a financial one. The complaint about these ventures is their high managerial cost. The difference between this option and the others discussed here is that only in this one does the technology dependent parent not have clear managerial control of the operation. Major decisions in such a venture have to be made via negotiation and compromise, and the managerial time demanded by a 50–55 percent venture is very high. Many firms will not enter joint ventures of this type.

The model below results from the arguments presented thus far, and also reflects the belief that firms should be more conservative as the financial investment which they are making in their diversification rises. That is, if the diversification involves a small capital outlay, the firm might risk a less strong link with its technology supplier. Thus, in Figure 5, it is recommended that a firm planning a small scale, closely related diversification, choose a current or current and future technology agreement, whereas a large scale, closely related diversification should be implemented via a current and future technology license or a majority joint venture.

The boundaries shown in Figure 5 between the four types of agreements are not intended to be exact. They have been constructed on the principle that as a

## Figure 5
### PRESCRIPTIVE MODEL

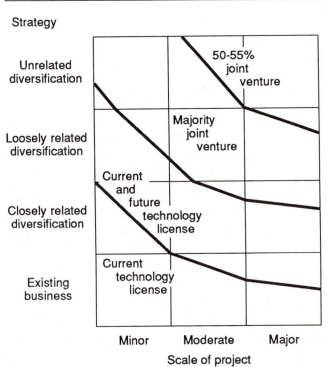

project increases in scale and degree of diversification, the necessary strength of relationship between the parties increases, and the type of agreement specified reflects this. The following sections address the question of whether or not firms actually behave as this model states that they should.

## Licensing Practice

Data on 74 license agreements involving Canadian and British licenses presented in Figure 6 suggest that firms do behave much as the model predicts they ought to. With the exception of the fact that some firms are using license agreements to pursue unrelated diversification, a phenomenon to be discussed in a moment, the data are approximately what one would expect. As the degree of diversification increases, so does the proportion of current and future technology agreements. In the simplest situations, small and moderate expansions using existing skills, no current and future technology agreements are being used at all. To implement loosely related diversification, many more firms are using current and future agreements rather than current agreements, and few license agreements are used at all in projects of any magnitude. The only surprise is that firms are using current technology agreements to effect closely related diversification.

A close examination was made of the license agreements used in unrelated diversification situations. It was found that in the largest of these projects the licensees had taken unusual steps to increase the strength of the bond with the licensor.

### Figure 6
#### LICENSING DATA

| | Investment ($000's) | | | |
|---|---|---|---|---|
| | **<50** | **50–499** | **500 +** | **Totals** |
| Unrelated | $c = 0$ <br> $c + f = 0$ | $c = 2$ <br> $c + f = 0$ | $c = 0$ <br> $c + f = 2$ | $c = 2$ <br> $c + f = 2$ |
| Loosely related | $c = 1$ <br> $c + f = 28$ | $c = 1$ <br> $c + f = 2$ | $c = 0$ <br> $c + f = 2$ | $c = 2$ <br> $c + f = 32$ |
| Closely related | $c = 1$ <br> $c + f = 3$ | $c = 4$ <br> $c + f = 5$ | $c = 7$ <br> $c + f = 2$ | $c = 12$ <br> $c + f = 10$ |
| Existing product | $c = 5$ <br> $c + f = 0$ | $c = 6$ <br> $c + f = 0$ | $c = 1$ <br> $c + f = 2$ | $c = 12$ <br> $c + f = 2$ |
| Totals | $c = 7$ <br> $c + f = 31$ | $c = 13$ <br> $c + f = 7$ | $c = 8$ <br> $c + f = 8$ | $c = 28$ <br> $c + f = 46$ |

*Note:* $c$ = current technology agreement
$c + f$ = current and future technology agreement

In one case, the licensee stipulated that a senior executive of the licensor must come to work for the Canadian firm for a period of two years, to be replaced by a fellow worker when this term expired. This was the only one of the 74 agreements in which such a transaction took place. In the other large unrelated project, the two companies were situated in immediately adjacent cities on either side of the Canada-U.S. border. Telephone communication between the firms took place, right down to the level of draftsman. Many problems were solved over a downtown lunch. These examples seem to reinforce the underlying principle on which Figure 5 was constructed.

## Use of Joint Ventures _____

The sample of joint ventures which was available for examination, the 28 shown in Figure 7, is significantly smaller than that used to examine licensing practices, but is large enough to demonstrate conclusively that the model of Figure Five does not accurately predict the situations in which firms will use the two types of joint ventures in question.[4] Joint ventures in which the technology dependent partner held 50–55 percent of the equity were commonly used in situations in which it was predicted that only current and future technology agreements or majority joint ventures would be used. On the other hand, only one firm attempted a large scale, unrelated diversification using a 50–55 percent joint venture, which was the application for which

**Figure 7**

**JOINT VENTURE DATA**

| | Investment ($000's) | | | |
| | < 50 | 50–499 | 500 + | Totals |
|---|---|---|---|---|
| Unrelated | | | 50/55 = 1 | 50/55 = 1 |
| | 0 | 0 | MAJ = 0 | MAJ = 0 |
| Loosely related | 50/55 = 1 | 50/55 = 6 | 50/55 = 3 | 50/55 = 10 |
| | MAJ = 0 | MAJ = 0 | MAJ = 2 | MAJ = 2 |
| Closely related | 50/55 = 2 | 50/55 = 4 | 50/55 = 5 | 50/55 = 11 |
| | MAJ = 0 | MAJ = 0 | MAJ = 2 | MAJ = 2 |
| Existing product | | | 50/55 = 1 | 50/55 = 1 |
| | 0 | 0 | MAJ = 1 | MAJ = 1 |
| Totals | 50/55 = 3 | 50/55 = 10 | 50/55 = 10 | 50/55 = 23 |
| | MAJ = 0 | MAJ = 0 | MAJ = 5 | MAJ = 5 |

*Notes:* (i) 50/55 denotes a joint venture in which the technology dependent firm owns between 50 and 55 percent.
(ii) MAJ denotes a joint venture in which the technology dependent firm owns 70 percent or more.

it was expected most such ventures would be used. Another striking observation was that only five of the 28 were majority joint ventures.

These surprising results could simply be the result of a biased sample, but this sample is believed to be appropriate to the questions under consideration. Each of the 28 ventures included one firm which needed technology, and another which supplied it. Most were international and involved Canadian, American, or West European firms. Ventures in which one partner played the role of a passive investor were avoided, as were those which were actually nothing more than incomplete takeovers with the original owner still holding a portion of the equity. Thus, the sample held some biases, but they were such as to make it more appropriate to the investigation at hand, not less.

It was discovered through further questioning that the underlying cause of both the relatively low use of majority joint ventures and the seemingly inappropriate use of 50–55 percent joint ventures was the same. *Many firms with valuable technology will not supply it to a joint venture in which they own less than 50 percent.* Thus, the market contains a significant discontinuity. Many technology seeking firms try to set up joint ventures in which they will be the majority owner, but are offered only 50–50 joint ventures. Faced with no other choice, or perhaps only an opportunity to enter an equally inappropriate license agreement, firms opt for the 50–50 joint venture. Thus, the frequent use of ventures in the 50–50 percent category in situations in which less strong linkages seems to be called for, is explained.

## The Market for Technology

In the process of talking with managers of both technology dependent firms and technology suppliers, in an effort to understand the results in Figure Seven, a number of factors emerged concerning the market for technology. The overwhelming impression is of a small, fragmented, inconsistent market in which both buyers and sellers operate with little information. Several characteristics of the market which seem particularly relevant to managers of firms wishing to buy technology are discussed below.

### The High Cost of Search

The major companies in an industry do not, as a general rule, want to sell their technology. They might sell technology in a fringe area into which they ventured by chance, but they would usually rather capture for themselves the return on technology relating to their major businesses. This means that their preference is to serve a foreign market through exports or direct foreign investment, to the extent that this is feasible considering the economics of the situation and the attitude of the foreign government involved. The implications for a potential technology purchaser is that it will have to look among the smaller firms in the industry, and at firms in different industries to find willing technology suppliers.[5] This does not result in an easy search process. It is made more difficult by the fact that many firms with good technology which they would be willing to sell, do not consider the sale of information to be a particularly lucrative activity, and thus do not advertise their position, or even make it particularly easy for a buyer to negotiate a sale. They have more important things to worry about. Thus, the size and nature of the market is determined by the thoroughness and aggressiveness of the potential purchaser. The difficult decision which managers often face is whether to accept the deal they are currently being offered, which does not quite fit their needs, or to keep on with the search.

## Disparate Choices

If a firm is persistent in its search for a supplier of technology, it may well end up with several very dissimilar offers for obtaining the same technology. In 1977, a Canadian firm was attempting a loosely related diversification of moderate scale—a situation which according to Figure Five would call for a majority joint venture, or possibly a current and future technology agreement. However, one European firm offered the Canadians a current technology agreement with a royalty rate of 2–3 percent of sales, while a second suggested a 50–50 joint venture in which the partner would supply machinery (rather than cash) as equity, and would provide two executives for the joint venture. Neither choice was ideal, in the Canadians' view; one offering too much liaison with the technology supplier, and the other not enough. However, because the firm felt it needed more help than was available with the current technology license agreement, it chose the joint venture. A Canadian competitor subsequently picked up the license agreement. Two years later, the joint venture was liquidated, a victim in part of the lack of flexibility caused by having a partner thousands of miles away who needed to be consulted on decisions which the market demanded be made quickly. The competitor with the license agreement has flourished.

The most difficult choice of supplier appears to arise in situations in which the quality of the technology varies between two suppliers, as well as the price and administrative mechanism (license agreement of joint venture) demanded. A typical example would be one in which the firm with what appears to be the better technology will only supply it to a 50–50 joint venture, and demands a higher price for it. The firm with the weaker technology is more flexible and offers a lower price. The buyer's indecision is often compounded by the fact that it is not completely confident of its assessment of the relative merits of the two technologies.

## Price is Negotiable

Neither buyers nor sellers of technology seem to have a clear idea of the value of the commodity in which they are trading. A European firm recently asked to be given 40 percent of the equity of a new North American joint venture to which it was supplying technology. The North American manager was not at all certain what the European technology was worth, but decided to make a counter offer of 15 percent. The negotiation ended when both sides agreed on a final figure of 20 percent. This reduction from 40 percent to 20 percent on the part of the technology supplier was very significant, as this was not a small joint venture. Another example of the uncertainty surrounding the price of technology was provided in the mid 1970s when a major U.S. company was trying to attract partners into a joint venture in which it would supply the technology. The approach of this billion dollar company was to say, "Here is the work we have done over the past 10 years, what do you think it is worth?" At least one new entrant was astounded by this procedure, observing that if the creator of the technology could not put a value on it, how did they expect outsiders to do so?

Another sign of the confusion in the market is that current and future technology license agreements, which appear to offer more to the licensee, do not carry higher royalty rates. The following data were collected from British licensees by the author in 1976.

A second test was carried out to see if royalty rates were a function of product age or of the uniqueness of the technology. They were not, leading one to speculate that royalty rates may be simply a function of negotiating skills of the parties involved.

## Implications for Technology Buyers

### Develop a Minimum Level of Technical Competence

To venture unprotected into an unstructured market like that described above is foolhardy. Even to function effectively as a technology buyer, a firm needs a certain technical competence. Otherwise it cannot begin to evaluate what it is being offered. Once a deal is signed, technical competence will again be useful in sorting out information coming from the technology supplier. One cannot simply accept uncritically all suggestions and technical specifications coming from a firm which may be a significantly different size than one's own, and located in a different country. Many technology purchasers also find that transfer of technical ideas is much more effective if they have on staff someone who is trained in the relevant discipline and thus "speaks the same language" as the engineer who is sending information from the supplying firm.

The successful Swedish joint venture referred to at the beginning of the paper had by 1980 built up a staff of 80 technicians and engineers. Their job was to scrutinize the information coming from the United States and to adapt it to best serve the needs of their particular operation. They were so successful at this that in some

**Figure 8**

**ROYALTY RATE AND LICENSE AGREEMENT TYPE**

| Royalty Rate | Current Technology | Current And Future Technology | Total |
|---|---|---|---|
| Less than 2% | 2 | 2 | 4 |
| 2 – 4.9% | 6 | 9 | 15 |
| 5 – 10% | 7 | 18 | 25 |
| More than 10% | 1 | 1 | 2 |
| Total | 16 | 30 | 46 |

years their operating performance was superior to that of the U.S. divisions which were supplying the technology. American visitors became a common sight in the Swedish plant, not only to teach, but also to learn the differences in operating procedure which had increased the Swedes' efficiency.

## Know Your Needs

When shopping in a market as diverse and unpredictable as that for technology, a firm should have a very good idea of just what it needs in the way of help. Is marketing assistance needed, or just production process specifications? What about product design changes in coming years? Can the firm keep up to date on its own or will it need continuing help from the technology supplier? As stated above, the firm looking for technology is likely to be offered alternatives with radically different costs and implications. Unless one is very well aware of his firm's strengths and weaknesses, and in particular its ability to learn with and without help, these choices will be very difficult.

In addition to being able to size up one's own firm, a manager should also be capable of assessing the character of a potential technology supplier. Is the firm used to transmitting its knowledge to others? Is it jealous of its technology or open with it? Will it be easy or difficult for your firm to gain the attention of employees of the technology supplier once the deal is made. Some managers explain that a joint venture, with senior members of the technology supplier on its board, can readily get the attention of division managers and engineers, whereas the same may not be true if the only link between buyer and seller is a license agreement.

## Consider the 50–50 Joint Venture

In the course of identifying the thirty joint ventures referred to in this study, the researcher interviewed over 100 managers in North America and Western Europe, to discuss their joint venture experiences.[5] One clear conclusion is that a great many managers, particularly in North America, will not enter 50–50 joint ventures. They view such ventures as too ambiguous, too inflexible, and all too likely to end in stalemated confusion and disaster. As the data in this paper suggest, however, any firm wishing to buy technology which arbitrarily decides that it will not enter 50–50 joint ventures is severely restricting its options. Fifty-five is as far as many firms with technology will go, in terms of allowing their local partner an equity holding.

One reason for the aversion to 50–50 ventures is that their potential difficulties are well known, and the tales of a few spectacular disasters are widespread. Less well known are the successes, and the considerable benefits which can accrue to a firm which is in an equal partnership with a world leader in the technology in question. The effort made by the technology supplier in such a situation to ensure that information is properly and completely transferred to the joint venture is equivalent to that which it would make for a wholly owned subsidiary. One leading German company spends $250,000 annually developing technology for, and supplying it to, a 50–50 joint venture in the United States. In addition it has supplied two fulltime managers to the venture, carries out training programs for American personnel both in Germany and the US, and on a monthly basis, sends news of competitors, new product applications, and tests of new products to the joint venture. There are a group of product specialists in Germany who are responsible for monitoring the joint venture's activities with respect to their product. In four years, the venture's sales have doubled to $80 million. The problems of managing a 50–50 joint venture can be significant, but so can the rewards. Firms seriously interested in buying technology cannot afford a "hands off" attitude to these ventures.

## Summary

Buying technology can be a viable corporate strategy. To use it effectively, a firm must have some minimum level of technical competence. The market is small and fragmented, and the deals which a technology seeking firm uncovers will be largely the result of its own hard work. Firms with technology that they would be willing to sell seldom advertise the fact. When deciding whether or not to enter a particular deal, a manager should have closely estimated the amount of help that will be needed in the new product area, and also should know the different degrees of access the company's employees will get to the supplier's personnel under various types of license agreements and joint ventures. To be successful, a manager needs to know his firm's requirements and have the perseverance to locate a supplier who can meet them.

Many firms with technology will not enter joint ventures in which they own less than 50 percent of the equity. This means that technology buyers may be faced with situations in which their only options are either a closer relationship with the technology supplier than they would ideally like, or no deal at all. Firms that wish to seriously pursue a strategy of technology acquisition need to develop the management skills necessary to handle 50–50 joint ventures.

## Notes

1. The skills concept of diversification is an outgrowth of the thesis of Leonard Wrigley, *Divisional Autonomy and Diversification,* Harvard Business School, unpublished Ph.D. thesis, 1970. For further elaboration, see Peter Killing, "Diversification Through Licensing," *R & D Management,* June, 1978.
2. Peter Killing, "Manufacturing Under License," *Business Quarterly,* Winter, 1977.
3. Howard Davies, "Technology Transfer Through Commercial Transaction," *Journal of Industrial Economics,* December, 1977.
4. The joint venture data were collected as part of an ongoing study on the management of joint ventures. The intended result is a book, *Managing Difficult Joint Ventures,* for which a 1981 publication is planned.
5. For similar observations, see Piero Telesio, *Licensing Policy in Multinational Enterprises,* unpublished Ph.D. thesis, Harvard University, 1978.

# III ___ PRACTICES _____

70

# 6. JAPANESE MANUFACTURING TECHNIQUES: THEIR IMPORTANCE TO U.S. MANUFACTURERS

**KIYOSHI SUZAKI**

*Kiyoshi Suzaki is a Managing Associate of Theodore Barry & Associates in Los Angeles.*

Advances made in manufacturing techniques are producing a revolution in competitive strategy. Improved production techniques not only affect quality control but reduce costs such as those associated with obsolescence and material handling. Executive managers can no longer afford to distance themselves from the functions of the factory floor.

United States manufacturers today cannot escape Japanese competition. Japan's superior quality control and special manufacturing techniques, such as "just-in-time" and *kanban,* are well recognized and widely discussed. Added to the omnipresent U.S. competitors, this relatively new rival for the consumer's hand is ample reason for U.S. manufacturers to be poised to meet and challenge such competition.

The role of manufacturing in a corporation changes and becomes more important as competition increases and the needs of consumers diversify. At the same time, the role of executive management is changing to meet the competition head on. Long estranged from that other world that functions on the factory floor, executive management historically has remained aloof, dealing with matters broad, strategic, and long-range. But in the race with competition, manufacturing provides the wheels that make the corporate vehicle move. To stay in the race, management must become much more involved in deciding which methods should be used to improve manufacturing capabilities.

The introduction of Japanese techniques into a U.S. manufacturing environment will not necessarily guarantee instant ascent to the top of the competitive heap. There is, however, so much evidence of dramatic productivity improvement and cost savings in those organizations where these techniques have been installed that it warrants very serious consideration. Even if management is not familiar with the "nuts and bolts" of the manufacturing operation, the importance of the role manufacturing plays in the organizational structure needs to be recognized and acknowledged.

A typical example of the impact special manufacturing techniques can have is illustrated in Exhibit 1. Between 1975 and 1980, a Japanese manufacturer of diesel engines discovered that defect rates and days of inventory were dramatically reduced, while real output per factory worker greatly increased. This was accomplished even

## Exhibit 1
### IMPACT OF SPECIAL MANUFACTURING TECHNIQUES ON JAPANESE DIESEL ENGINE MANUFACTURER

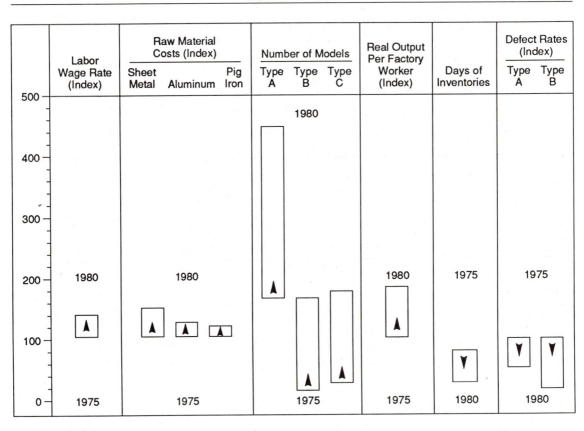

with a large increase in the number of models produced and while the labor wage rate and costs of raw materials increased.

But how many in management recognize the fundamental economic reasoning and strategic impact of Japanese manufacturing techniques? How many of those who actually take steps to incorporate these techniques incorporate them *correctly?* How many still consider them impossible to use in the United States because of cultural, geographical, and other differences?

The difficulty in understanding Japanese manufacturing techniques can be compared with a blind person touching an elephant; each set of issues may be observed and analyzed, yet the total picture or impact is hard to grasp. As a result, it is difficult to install such techniques and achieve the benefit of their full potential. Therefore, the approach must be *incremental* for implementation to be successful, with sequential steps building up to each component. These components are then combined and fine-tuned into an integrated system. Correctly installed, they result in an interrelated manufacturing system where all of the components are mutually dependent.

## Bias Toward Action

Taiichi Ohno, known as the founder of the Toyota production system, emphasized that "bias toward action" is the key. In his words, "By actually trying, various problems become known. . . . As such problems gradually became clear, they taught me the direction of the next move."

With this philosophy, Toyota took about twenty to thirty years to develop its efficient production system. A company should need no more than two years to develop the system—*if* certain steps are followed and *if* senior management's involvement and commitment are gained. The development process is similar to that at Toyota, but the basic work has already been accomplished.

## Rapid Tool-Setting

Rapid tool-setting or minimum-setup-time operation is an absolute requirement in implementing Japanese manufacturing techniques. By cutting down the setup time, not only are machine downtime and work-in-process (WIP) reduced, but so are the costs associated with obsolescence, materials handling, materials control, and quality control. These cost savings more than offset the costs incurred in reducing setup time. Exhibit 2 illustrates the astounding improvements that rapid tool-setting has produced in four Japanese and two U.S. manufacturing companies.

Hundreds of similar cases have proved that setup times can be reduced to ten minutes or less, that is, an improvement factor of twenty or more. At the same time, WIP levels have been reduced dramatically and other improvements have been achieved. A "break the old habit" attitude, with a fresh perspective and strong persistence, is the fundamental requirement in achieving rapid tool-setting.

Other improvements include increased safety, simpler operation, higher yield, and increased flexibility for emergency work. Such visible achievement will boost worker morale, triggering improvement in other areas. With rapid tool-setting, the notion of economic order quantity is changed and small-lot production becomes possible and economical.

Even though certain steps are necessary to achieve rapid tool-setting, such as converting off-stream setting to on-stream setting and eliminating unnecessary adjustments, the key is to (1) firmly believe it is possible, and (2) pursue its achievement.

## Smooth Transportation

In most job-shop operations in the United States, a functional department layout still seems to be the most common. For example, lathes are clustered in the factory and operated by workers specializing in such skills. This contrasts with a layout oriented to production flow, where equipment is in line with material flow—the common approach in Japan.

When a lot size is big, it is cost-effective to carry large amounts of parts at once—with forklifts. But when the lot size is small, transportation required to reach each succeeding process is inevitably increased. The most effective solution to this

## Exhibit 2
### FACTORY IMPROVEMENT—RAPID TOOL-SETTING

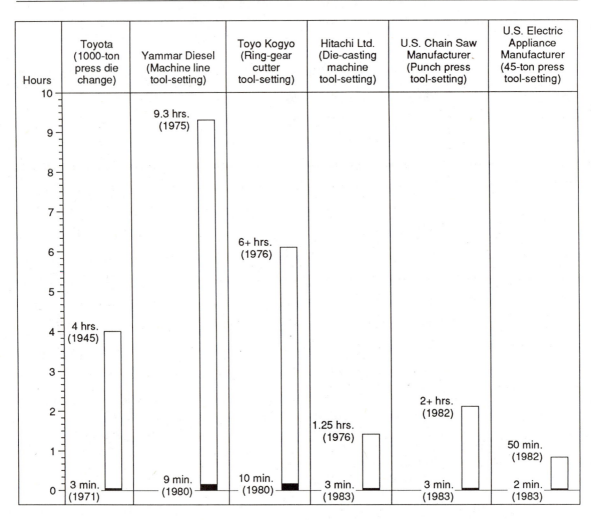

| Hours | Toyota (1000-ton press die change) | Yammar Diesel (Machine line tool-setting) | Toyo Kogyo (Ring-gear cutter tool-setting) | Hitachi Ltd. (Die-casting machine tool-setting) | U.S. Chain Saw Manufacturer (Punch press tool-setting) | U.S. Electric Appliance Manufacturer (45-ton press tool-setting) |
|---|---|---|---|---|---|---|
| | 4 hrs. (1945) | 9.3 hrs. (1975) | 6+ hrs. (1976) | 1.25 hrs. (1976) | 2+ hrs. (1982) | 50 min. (1982) |
| | 3 min. (1971) | 9 min. (1980) | 10 min. (1980) | 3 min. (1983) | 3 min. (1983) | 2 min. (1983) |

problem for the Japanese was to change the plant layout and adopt a convenient transporting method, such as the chute or hand pushcart.

At Toyo Kogyo, for example, improvements in tool-setting, layouts, and procedures for the machining operation of steering knuckles have reduced the number of workers by about 60 percent and WIP inventory by more than 90 percent.

By changing plant layout and adopting a convenient transportation system with rapid tool-setting, factory floor space will be utilized more efficiently, usually by a factor of two or more. The number of forklifts required will be significantly reduced; furthermore, such change shortens the production period, or time-in-plant period, by a factor of at least two. Exhibit 3 illustrates the advantages of an improved system for simplified materials flow.

**Exhibit 3**
## IMPROVED MATERIALS FLOW

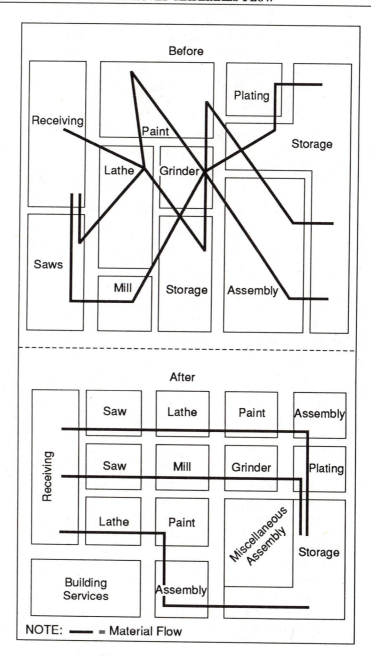

## Machine Utilization

By modifying the production layout, and consequently improving transportation flow, machine utilization rates are reduced because machines are dedicated to specific material flows. Several approaches may be used to solve this problem, but the basic principle to remember is: *Produce only the quantity required.*

One approach is to produce similar products through the same line. The ability of rapid tool-setting will help utilize machines for "bypass operation" to take advantage of otherwise idle capacity.

Another approach is to acquire, or even self-manufacture, equipment that fits the process. The idea is to utilize low-cost conventional machines rather than install very sophisticated multipurpose machines.

A third approach is to focus on labor productivity, rather than machine productivity, by utilizing multimachine handling.

After all, the loss in machine utilization must be measured against the gains from shortened production periods, reduced WIP levels, and reduced direct and indirect costs. Generally, it is preferable to sacrifice machine utilization for these gains. Maximizing the use of workers is more important than maximizing the use of machines. This is because (1) direct labor has leverage effects on indirect labor cost; (2) machine cost, when depreciated over years, is usually cheaper than labor cost; and (3) machine cost is a sunk cost anyway.

## Autonomation/Multimachine Handling

It has long been widely accepted that a worker must always stand by a machine in operation. But with equipment designed to stop automatically and emit signals when the required quantity has been produced or when defects occur, there is no need for the worker to stand by the machine. Toyota calls this *autonomation*—as opposed to automation, where the machine does not have such capabilities.

With autonomation, machines are separated from workers—and a worker can operate more than one machine. This is called a *multimachine-handling* operation. Change in layout and fluctuation of production volume and product mix may require a worker to operate different kinds of machines, such as punch presses, lathes, and milling machines. Such an operation is called *multiprocess handling.*

Since these operations convert a worker's waiting time into productive working time, productivity gains of more than 30 percent to 50 percent are normally achieved. In the United States, however, such processes may create labor opposition, whereas workers in Japan have simply adapted to the change, either for the survival of the company or for their own benefit. A worker from one of the major Japanese automobile companies commented, "I see acquiring many skills as a requirement for promotion. If I can handle more machines or robots, that means I am more valuable to my company."

*By changing plant layout and adopting a convenient transportation system, factory floor space will be utilized more efficiently, usually by a factor of two or more.*

In fact, that is how pay scales are developed at Matsushita and many other companies in Japan. To give an example of multiprocess handling, at Toyota's engine-assembly operation, one worker was observed who handled thirty-five production processes. It took him eight minutes, twenty-six second (± two seconds) for one round of processes and he totaled six miles of walking a day.

Toyota adopted multimachine/multiprocess handling operations about thirty years ago when, on average, one worker operated five sets of machines. But it is difficult to break old habits. One major Japanese construction-equipment manufacturer adopted the new layout concept and multimachine/multiprocess handling just three to five years ago—about twenty-five years later than Toyota. However, these practices made it possible to reduce the work force or the cost of production significantly, sometimes more than 30 percent for typical machine-shop operations.

By having workers take charge of multiple machines and a wider range of functions, they become able to cope with the fluctuating production volume and the diversified product mix.

## Poka Yoke: A Foolproof Mechanism

T. Ishihara, President of Nissan Motor Company, commented at the International Productivity Conference in 1983, "The 'synchronized' system will not work unless the parts produced by the supplier are 100 percent guaranteed for quality and can be directly supplied to the automaker without an acceptance inspection. No confusion resulting from parts defects can be allowed in the auto production line."

This concept may seem impossible to Western manufacturers. It *is* achievable, however, and without much cost—but it takes careful planning. As in the auton-omation concept, where the machine stops and gives signals automatically when any abnormal situation occurs, *poka yoke* (which roughly translates to "a foolproof mech-anism") is incorporated in devices to prevent inadvertent or negligent actions by workers. For example, such devices may reject defective parts or stop the machine when a part is improperly set up or when there are errors in operating procedures.

The key is to *prevent* defects rather than to rely on the inspection line to detect them. With *poka yoke* in place, there should be no defective parts carried to the subsequent process; theoretically, then, no inspection is needed at the end of the line, no rework is needed, and there is no materials waste.

Because of the lack of such practices, U.S. companies have from three to fifteen times more inspectors than their Japanese counterparts—but they still produce five times more defective parts!

## Small-Lot Production

Small-lot production is synonymous with nonstock production of minimum-time-in-plant production. When such production becomes possible, setup times, transportation times, and WIP inventories are minimized; machines are balanced; and the factory becomes almost like a continuous processing plant or oil refinery. It is similar to a free-flowing freeway, in contrast with metropolitan streets with heavy traffic jams, where slow-moving vehicles and reckless drivers can clog the system.

The first step in trying to install a small-lot production system is to designate stock points and containers to hold WIP inventories. Then, set goals to reduce WIP levels, such as cutting WIP levels by 50 percent in the next year. Senior management's involvement and commitment are mandatory for successful implementation.

As inventory levels start to go down, new bottlenecks will surface—such as the need to further reduce the setup time of a machine, to change the layout for smoother transportation, or to put more *poka yoke* devices in place. When these bottlenecks are removed and the goals met, new goals for the next year will be posted (e.g., cut the WIP level by 50 percent again). This chaining process stimulates ideas for improvement, rather than maintaining the status quo.

As the WIP levels go down, the production period is shortened. This leads to early detection of defects because of quick feedback from downstream processes. Communication in the factory is improved and different work centers become integrated with tighter coupling. On the other hand, machine breakdown becomes a serious problem when the WIP level is low; hence *preventive maintenance becomes very important.* When workers start to pay more attention to their machines and their jobs, they often learn to handle small maintenance jobs and to produce higher-quality work.

When a machine or a worker is in trouble, such information is either automatically or manually transmitted through *andon,* an information-transfer device made of a light panel designed for trouble reporting. *Andon* provides a means for early warning and quick recovery, and may be considered a modified version of *poka yoke.* When these concepts are implemented, the impact is significant. Small-lot production brings different techniques into one integrated system. And the results are a shorter production period, higher quality, and higher productivity—without much capital expenditure.

For example, Toyota reduced its production period from fifteen days to one day. Nissan and Toyo Kogyo had similar results. At the same time, these three automobile manufacturers found that every time the WIP level halved relative to production volume, labor productivity was increased—about 40 percent over a ten-year period. Exhibit 4 illustrates this correlation.

Japanese manufacturers of motorcycles, electronic products, and auto parts reported that, in the span of two to three years, production times were cut by 20–50 percent, WIP inventories were reduced 20–40 percent, and labor productivity was increased by 50–80 percent.

Exhibit 5 illustrates the improved production lead time experienced by two Japanese and two U.S. manufacturers. In the case of Matsushita, washing machine production time was reduced from fifteen days to an astonishing two and one-half hours. This was accompanied by significant productivity and quality improvement.

In the United States, a motor-control manufacturer reduced production time from eight weeks to one week. At the same time, the inventory level was halved, floor space was halved, and indirect labor costs were reduced significantly. Such impressive results have had a strong impact on the long-term direction in which these companies are headed; this is also true of many others who have experienced similar results. Again, senior management's involvement and commitment should be gained early in the efforts to make these things happen.

## Exhibit 4
### PRODUCTIVITY AND WIP

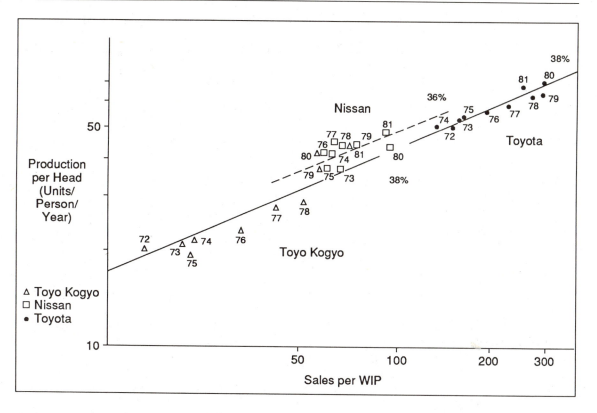

## Leveled Production/Mixed Production

When small-lot production becomes possible, further reduction of WIP inventories is achieved by *leveled production*—running a same-level, uniform schedule every day, with different product types mixed together. A leveled work load enables workers to concentrate on their jobs, resulting in more efficient operation. *Mixed production* means the lowest limit of small-lot production at the leveled schedule.

When achieved, this will bring a smooth flow of parts and even work loads throughout the factory. Unnecessary expediting, checking, rework, and delays are minimized, as are the finished product and WIP inventories. At this point the factory starts to run like a process plant, and "just-in-time" production—where a part arrives at a work center or assembly line at just the instant it is needed—is within reach.

## Production Control System

According to the nature of the business and its current production patterns, it is necessary to choose the most suitable production control system. Systems should

## Exhibit 5
### FACTORY IMPROVEMENT PRODUCTION LEAD TIME

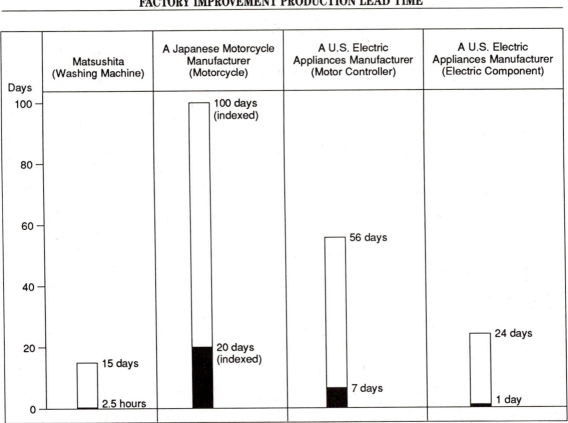

be developed according to the overall demand profile, number of product models, and the degree of repetition. Certain trade-offs need to be resolved among manufacturing, marketing, and other functions. For example, smoothing production volume needs to be compensated with delivery time of certain items when demands fluctuate.

Material requirements planning (MRP) may be suitable in many instances, but the world-renowned *kanban* system, developed by Toyota, might be the better choice when demands do not fluctuate rapidly.

When using *kanban,* a piece of paper is attached to the work piece showing part number, part name, quantity, storage place, etc. With this used as the information system, parts are produced or delivered just before they are needed, serving as a tool to achieve just-in-time production.

In order to make the *kanban* system effective, however, it is necessary to control production schedules more rigidly. At Toyota, daily production is determined ten to twenty days in advance and no modification is permitted afterwards.

While this scheduling might limit the ability to cope with change in demand, the Kanban system can save indirect costs associated with inventory and production control. To illustrate, there are about five times more indirect workers in U.S. automobile manufacturing than in the Japanese equivalent using *kanban*. The system also serves as a means to decrease inventory further by reducing the number of *kanbans* or container capacities and therefore generates vast improvements.

Just as there is no organizational structure that suits all situations, there is no production control system that suits all businesses. When business characteristics do not fit well, the application of such a system may result in failure; but even when it does fit well, the system will not work unless correct approaches are taken. There are examples of MRP or *kanban* misuse that resulted in disasters—caused either by mismatching business characteristics or by taking the wrong approach, such as implementing the systems without making improvements to the production processes. But when carefully studied and integrated with other approaches, such systems can bring vast improvements, as evidenced by many Japanese successes.

Even though some of the basic steps in a typical improvement program are interrelated, they are for the most part sequential:

1. Start with rapid tool-setting.
2. Smooth the transportation.
3. Assess machine utilization to increase gains in costs/lead time.
4. Implement autonomation and multimachine handling.
5. Put *poka yoke* in place.
6. Cut WIP levels to achieve small-lot production.
7. Introduce leveled and mixed production to smooth production flow.
8. Develop a production control system to achieve just-in-time production.

## Use Creative Thinking: Not Money

The techniques described do not require much capital expenditure. The point is to expose the bottlenecks, understand basic principles, and "Use Creative Thinking: Not Money."

A study conducted in Japanese automobile companies revealed that 70 percent of total productivity improvement comes from improving manufacturing on the factory floor, and the remaining 30 percent results from expenditures on capital equipment such as robots and numerically controlled machine tools. Even in high-growth businesses such as electric typewriters and printers, or mature businesses such as refrigerators and room air-conditioners, about half of productivity improvement comes from improvement at the factory floor level.

American managements need to devote special attention to manufacturing techniques. This will happen only through the recognition of how *much* improvement in productivity and profit is made possible through the use of competitive manufacturing techniques. Although the bulk of improvement may come from engineering efforts, management should also consider ways to motivate and involve blue-collar workers. Japanese companies have succeeded in increasing the involvement of these previously underutilized workers through activities such as "quality circles," suggestion programs, and miscellaneous educational programs. Such programs can help improve worker morale. Workers with self-thinking and self-controlling capabilities strengthen a company's manufacturing capabilities.

A significant difference in the utilization of worker resources in the United States and Japan can be seen when one looks at the fact that in the United States, the average number of suggestions per person per year is 0.15, and the adoption rate is 24 percent. In Japan, the average number of suggestions per person per year is 12.8, and the adoption rate is 72 percent.

## Conclusion

The advances being made in manufacturing techniques are producing a revolution in competitive strategy. Manufacturing will play a different role within itself and in its relation to other corporate functions.

If a business is already facing stiff Japanese competition, the manufacturing techniques of the competitors should be carefully studied—because most of the Japanese competitive advantages come from the way they manufacture products. It may also face stiffer U.S. competition if domestic competitors are already ahead in incorporating progressive manufacturing techniques.

It took twenty to thirty years for Toyota to achieve its efficient operation; about five years for other Japanese companies. But a company should be able to achieve the bulk of improvement in one or two years. The time to start is now—the game is changing, and management must play by new rules in order to stay in the game.

# 7. INTEGRATION OF INFORMATION SYSTEMS IN MANUFACTURING

**ARNOUD DE MEYER and KASRA FERDOWS**

*Received October 1984*
*Revised January 1985*

*The value of storing manufacturing data electronically has been widely accepted in industry. The combination of an expanding catalogue of software and less expensive hardware is making more comprehensive and integrated management communication systems technically feasible and economically justifiable. The benefits essentially stem from constructing a common database which contains a company's historical and up-to-date manufacturing information, and making this database easily accessible to all its potential users. The users might be in production, engineering, sales, marketing, distribution, finance, personnel, or other functions in the company. They could also be top management. Each user can add relevant data to the database and have rapid access to the latest information needed for preparing own reports. As such, all users have access to an integrated set of data which is internally consistent and is updated simultaneously for everyone. There are, clearly, great possibilities.*

*But how are the manufacturing companies around the globe reacting to these promises? Specifically, what are the areas on which they are concentrating their efforts? The purpose of this article is to address these questions. In answering these questions we rely primarily on the results of a recent survey of 560 manufacturers in Europe, North America, and Japan. There are intriguing singularities and differences in the three regions.*

## Introduction

Most early computerised information systems in manufacturing were reflections of the manual processing, planning and control systems in which each application or task was processed separately by use of separate files. Thus, systems for inventory control, production planning, scheduling and control, shop floor control, logistics, or quality assurance were usually developed separately and were built up around their own files. The separation of databases was even more pronounced for the computer supported links between manufacturing and engineering (e.g., with early computer aided design systems) or with accounting and finance.

Thanks to the increasing capacity and performance of computers of all sizes—from micros to big mainframes—we are now witnessing a distinct trend towards integration of information systems within manufacturing as well as between manufacturing and other functional areas in the company. The various islands of automated

Arnoud De Meyer and Kasra Ferdows, "Integration of Information Systems in Manufacturing." *International Journal of Operations and Production Management.* 5.2 (1985) 5–12. Reprinted by permission.

information processing and decision support systems are being continuously integrated to form broader systems. A clear starting point has been the introduction of materials requirements planning software packages which reconcile demand management with resource availability to plan long-term and short-term capacities and schedule production runs[1]. Subsequent steps to integrate information systems within areas directly related to manufacture, however, do not seem to follow a clear pattern: some of the systems seem to focus on reporting the productivity of people and machines, some on quality, some on maintenance, some on procurement, and some on the efficiency of the various stages of production process. Integration of all these systems within the manufacturing function is clearly an outstanding challenge[2].

In linking with other functions, the pattern of integration seems to vary rather substantially. The more recent manufacturing software packages also produce a limited number of financial reports (e.g., billing, payables, costing, inventory evaluation, capital budgeting, investment audit). But, in spite of the fact that the origin for many of the financial transactions is essentially in manufacturing (e.g., orders produced, materials used, labour hours spent, etc.) the full integration of databases for the finance and manufacturing functions does not seem to be widespread yet. This presents another challenge.

Sales and marketing, too, provide a great deal of input to the manufacturing database, and routinely need quick access. But organisational considerations seem to dictate the sort of software which is put in place for facilitating these transactions. The issues here are:

(a) to what extent marketing and sales data can be fed to the manufacturing database, (e.g., at the extreme, actual sales at the retail level are fed to the manufacturing database on a real-time basis), and

(b) to what extent sales and marketing can access the common manufacturing database and effect changes, (e.g., at the extreme, promise a delivery-date to a customer and schedule the order directly on the production schedule).

Such integrated information systems are likely to put the organisation on uncharted courses. This poses yet another challenge—one with exciting possibilities[3].

Integration of design, engineering, and production databases poses a somewhat different challenge. The emphasis here is to provide primarily technical information for technical people. The emphasis in many of the above systems, in contrast, is to provide managerial information. Perhaps this is one reason why in many companies there exist sophisticated design and engineering databases and separate, equally sophisticated, manufacturing databases, with almost no links between the two. Not being a primary customer, top management might have felt the benefits of such complex data integration would not justify its cost. The exceptions are found in those industries where technical reasons dictate the link (e.g., design and manufacture of microprocessors), or the technical advantages are easy to see and valued greatly (e.g., aerospace industry). The challenge here is to be imaginative in transforming the technical advantages which such linking of databases offer into competitive advantages in the marketplace.

Together, these are among the principal challenges on the road which leads to Computer-Integrated-Manufacture (CIM).

Though one might be able to design ideal CIM systems and envisage automated factories, it will undoubtedly take a lot of effort to get from the present-day dispersed systems to some level of integration[4]. In most of the cases one may assume that integrated information systems will be developed incrementally. Operations management and the information groups have to take difficult and far-reaching decisions on how to plan integration[5,6,7].

To support these decisions it is helpful to understand which integration paths other companies have decided to pursue. The results of the survey described below can provide useful insights.

## The Survey

Since 1982 an annual survey of large manufacturers in Europe, North America and Japan has been administered by means of a questionnaire issued by three research institutions in the following regions: INSEAD, Fontainebleau, France (where the authors conduct the European Survey), Boston University, Boston, USA (where J. G. Miller and T. E. Vollmann conduct the North American Survey) and Waseda University, Tokyo, Japan (where J. Nakane conducts the Japanese Survey). The purpose of the survey is to develop a database on a variety of issues relevant to manufacturing management in each region, and to make triad comparisons of the trends in the three regions[1].

The data presented in this article come from the 1984 survey in which about 560 manufacturers participated. One hundred and fifty-two of them were located in the UK, France, Germany, Belgium, Italy, Spain, Sweden, The Netherlands, Switzerland, Denmark and Norway; 214 were in North America (United States and Canada), and 198 in Japan. The executives who answered the questionnaires were mostly senior manufacturing managers, or were at a high level in the organisation. They represented a wide variety of industries, including food products, chemicals, machinery, electrical equipment, electronics, and automotive assembly. None of the industries represents more than 20 per cent of the sample.

Several questions in the questionnaire were related to the subject of this article. Some of them were aimed at gauging the overall emphasis that the company was placing on the integration of information systems within manufacturing and across functions. Other questions sought details of the pattern of integration of information sub-systems during the current and next two years.

### Results and Discussion

The first question which arises is whether integration of information systems is perceived to be of high priority by the respondents. Out of a list of 39 specific actions related to a broad variety of issues in operations management, the respondents could check into which of these they had put effort in the past year, and into which they planned to put effort in the next two years. Integrating manufacturing information systems and integrating information systems across functions were two of the actions out of the list of 39. Table 1 shows the rank order of these two actions for past and future efforts.

Integration of manufacturing systems was eighth on the list of past efforts for the European respondents, but has climbed to the fourth place for future efforts. The rise of integration across functions is even more spectacular: from seventeenth to fifth place. The North American and Japanese data show the same trend. In all three regions manufacturers are placing more emphasis on the integration of information systems. However, in a relative sense, the Japanese are placing less priority on these activities than Europeans and Americans. They either have other priorities or they may be concentrating on the development of the information sub-systems—such as for production and inventory control—first, before they venture into broader integration projects.

Nevertheless, there is little doubt that in all three regions more management attention is being paid to integration of information systems.

A second issue relates to the pattern of integration. Considering the multitude of information sub-systems which can be integrated within manufacturing, and between manufacturing and other functions, which ones are receiving more attention? Are there any differences between the three regions? A section of the questionnaire addressed this issue.

The section consisted of a multiple part question which asked what degree of emphasis the company intended to place in the next two years on better integration of a set of 21 information sub-systems. The list is shown in Table 2. The degree of emphasis was to be indicated on a continuous scale marked from no emphasis through small, moderate, significant, to critical emphasis. For the processing of the results, the answers were translated onto a linear scale ranging from ten to 50.

## Table 1
### PRIORITY OF INTEGRATION OF INFORMATION SYSTEMS

|  |  | (Rank Order On A List Of 39 Improvement Efforts) | | |
|  |  | Europe | North America | Japan |
|---|---|---|---|---|
| P A S T | Within Manufacturing | 8 | 7 | 25 |
|  | Across Functions | 17 | 20 | 36 |
| F U T U R E | Within Manufacturing | 4 | 3 | 10 |
|  | Across Functions | 5 | 9 | 27 |

**Table 2**

**COMPLETE LIST OF INFORMATION SYSTEMS
PRESENTED TO THE RESPONDENTS**

| | |
|---|---|
| Master Production Scheduling | Materials Requirements Planning |
| Inventory Status | Shop Floor Control |
| Purchasing | Design Engineering |
| Manufacturing Engineering | CAD |
| CAM | Process Control |
| Quality Control | Maintenance |
| Cost Accounting | Financial Performance Reporting |
| Budgeting | Strategic Planning |
| Order Entry | Sales Forecasting |
| Sales Planning and Analysis | Physical Distribution |
| Market Research | |

Table 3 shows the five information sub-systems ranked in order of preference which are receiving the highest emphasis for integration from the "typical" manufacturer in each region. Table 4 shows the five least emphasized sub-systems in each region.

Manufacturers in all three regions agree quite convincingly on the importance of integrating quality control data with other sub-systems. There seems also to be agreement on the importance of integration of the traditional production planning and control information sub-systems: materials requirements planning scores highly in Europe and North America and master production scheduling (which may or may not imply an MRP package) is high on the list of Japanese and Americans.

The differences in the three regions are, however, rather intriguing. The Europeans, on average, place quite an emphasis on the integration of sales related information systems. These same systems appear, however, in the Japanese data as the least emphasised for integration. The underlying pattern of the Japanese efforts can be characterised by an emphasis on the integration of process control information; rather different from Europe where integration of computer aided design and manufacture—two process related sub-systems—are at the bottom of the priority list, and rather closer to North America where the priority of shop floor and material flow controls are more pronounced.

In the Japanese list the high priority of cost accounting is also noteworthy (Table III). This might, at first sight, appear to contradict the relatively low rank given to the integration of the financial performance reporting (Table IV). One might, however, hypothesise that this reflects a bottom-up approach, starting on the shop floor and with the nuts and bolts of cost accounting, in contrast to a top-down approach, which would be reflected much more in the financial performance reporting.

The general picture which seems to emerge from the data is that, with respect to integration of information sub-systems, the Europeans seem to favour a top-down

## Table 3

## INFORMATION SUB-SYSTEMS WHICH ARE THE MOST EMPHASISED
## WITH RESPECT TO INTEGRATION

| Europe | US | Japan |
|---|---|---|
| Quality Control | Quality Control | Quality Control |
| Strategic Planning | Inventory Status | Cost Accounting |
| Sales Forecasting | Master Production Scheduling | Shop Floor Control |
| Sales Planning and Analysis | Materials Requirements Planning | Master Production Scheduling |
| Materials Requirements Planning | Shop Floor Control | Process Control |

approach, starting with strategic planning and sales-related issues, whereas the North American and Japanese favour a bottom-up approach, giving emphasis to down-to-earth shop floor control, inventory status and cost accounting. Typical in the Japanese results is the importance attached to integrating the technical side of the business with simple management systems, which might be a reflection of their continuous striving for marginal improvements in manufacturing[8].

A third issue is related to the co-variation among the variables: were there any significant relationships in the emphasis placed on the integration of these 21 sub-systems? For this issue, we analysed the European data only. A factor analysis was undertaken to try to find out along which dimensions the co-variance could be explained. Sixty-six per cent of the variance in the *total European* sample could be explained by six factors which are, in order of importance:

1. Sales forecasting and planning
2. Financial reporting and budgeting
3. Materials requirements planning
4. Process control
5. CAD and CAM
6. Design and manufacturing engineering

So, if one is looking for differences between European companies with respect to the emphasis they place on the integration of information systems, the most important factor is the one which is related to sales forecasting and planning. Some companies place a high emphasis on the integration of sales forecasting and control, whereas others pay far less attention to this. The same holds true, but in decreasing importance, for the five other factors.

It is interesting to note the characteristics of the companies which have placed high or low emphasis on each of these six factors. The questionnaire, in its entirety, provides enough data to draw a manufacturing profile of each of the companies and enables theoretically, manufacturing profiles to be suggested which place a high or low emphasis on each of these six factors. However, in this article these manufacturing profiles will be viewed as being tentative only, since the database of 152 companies in the European sample is rather small for this type of analysis. We could

**Table 4**

## INFORMATION SUB-SYSTEMS WHICH ARE LEAST EMPHASISED
## WITH RESPECT TO INTEGRATION

| Europe | US | Japan |
|---|---|---|
| CAD* | Physical Distribution* | Market Research* |
| CAM | Maintenance | Maintenance |
| Maintenance | Market Research | Financial Performance Reporting |
| Order Entry | Budgeting | Order Entry |
| Physical Distribution and Analysis | Order Entry | Sales Planning |

*Given lowest emphasis

not, moreover, control for the "noise" in the data, e.g., the influence of promotion campaigns of software houses in particular countries. Consequently the reader should see the following statements as suggestions to stimulate further enquiries on the topic. Having said this, the results of our analysis, as related to each of the six factors, can be summarised as follows:

1. Companies which emphasise, as competitive priorities, the ability to offer low prices, to make rapid design changes and consistent quality, put a high emphasis on the integration of sales forecasting and planning with other information sub-systems. It appears that low profit margins or markets characterised by rapid product design changes make good sales forecasting more crucial.

2. Integration of financial reporting and budgeting is emphasised by those companies which position themselves in the market on the basis of high performing products.

3. Integration of MRP systems is favoured by those companies that emphasise as competitive tools rapid design changes, consistent quality, the ability to offer products which provide a better performance than their competitors, and dependable delivery. Also of interest is that integration of MRP is emphasised by those companies pursuing product/market diversification. This might indicate that they hope to overcome the difficulty of MRP systems being able to cope with new products, by integrating more data from other information sub-systems into the MRP package.

4. Integration of process control is seen to be important by those companies with a production process which is close to continuous flow, but also by those that use fast delivery as a competitive tool.

5. Integration of CAD-CAM is related to the production of one-of-a-kind capital goods, and especially in those industries where competitive pricing is critical to success.

6. Integration of design and manufacturing engineering systems is emphasised by those business units that are trying to enter new markets with existing products (market diversification) and those that want to enter new markets by relying on products which perform better than the products in existing markets.

# Conclusion

Our survey of 560 manufacturing companies in Europe, North America and Japan supports the hypothesis that integration of information systems within manufacturing, and between manufacturing and other functions, is a growing concern. In all three regions management is paying increasing attention to this issue, although in Japan it does not appear to be yet as important, or receiving the same priority, as in the other two regions. Japanese manufacturers are probably still working on the development of individual components of an integrated information system.

The pattern of integration of the various information sub-systems, however, differs from region to region. The European respondents seem to favour more strongly a "top-down" approach, while the North American and Japanese respondents seem to prefer a "bottom-up" approach. In developing their integrated manufacturing information systems, the North Americans seem to be more concerned with control of materials flow, the Europeans with demand management. Japanese manufacturers are more concerned with technical and engineering issues. All three, however, are unanimous that the integration of quality related data with other information sub-systems carries a very high priority.

# References

1. Vollmann, T. E., Berry, W. L. and Whybark, D. C., *Manufacturing Planning and Control Systems,* Richard D. Irwin, 1984.
2. Mantz, R. K., Merten, A. G. and Severance, D. G., *Senior Management Control of Computer-Based Information Systems,* Financial Executive Research Foundation, 1983.
3. McFarlan, F. W., McKenny, J. L. and Pyburn, P., "The Information Archipelago— Plotting a Course", *Harvard Business Review,* January-February 1983.
4. "Manufacturing Technology: Tomorrow Comes to the Plant", *Dun's Business Month,* October 1984.
5. Ferdows, K. and De Meyer, A., "The State of Large Manufacturers in Europe: Results of the 1984 European Manufacturing Futures Survey", INSEAD, 1984.
6. Miller, J. G. and Vollmann, T. E., "The 1984 Manufacturing Futures Project: Summary of North American Responses", Boston University, 1984.
7. Nakane, J., "The 1984 Manufacturing Futures Project: Summary of Japan", Waseda University, 1984.
8. Hayes, R. H. and Wheelwright, S. C., *Restoring our Competitive Edge: Competing through Manufacturing,* John Wiley and Sons, 1984.

# 8. WORK IMPROVEMENT PROGRAMMES: QUALITY CONTROL CIRCLES COMPARED WITH TRADITIONAL WESTERN APPROACHES

**RICHARD J. SCHONBERGER**
*Department of Management, University of Nebraska-Lincoln*

*Quality control circles, a Japanese management technique for improving quality, productivity, and worker morale, have been widely adopted in western industry. The apparent hope is that the circles are a key to competing with the Japanese. In this paper QC circles are shown to resemble, and potentially overlap with, six other western work improvement programmes, most of which have had successful histories.*

*The issue of which programmes to implement in western work environments is indirectly examined by considering the approach of a Japanese plant operating in the United States. QC circles are not used. Instead, plant management has developed a work improvement programme employing a "vision" of the ideal physical plant configuration toward which the plant should continually evolve. The configuration facilitates a streamlined repetitive production line mode of operation that attempts to encompass subassembly and fabrication as well as final assembly processes.*

*The case observations offer limited evidence that plant configuration considerations should be foremost among the factors emphasised in an industrial work improvement programme and that western industry should not expect too much from quality control circles.*

Western visitors to Japanese industry have returned with numerous explanations for Japanese productivity and product quality. Prominent among these explanations are: frugality, industriousness, engineering emphasis in education, a long-term outlook (attributable to reliance on long-term debt), an educational emphasis on engineering, high savings and capital investment, company unions, and group-think/consensus mechanisms for work improvement. The common view is that frugality and industriousness are Japanese cultural traits and that the engineering emphasis and the debt/outlook condition are institutionalised in Japan. The remaining Japanese success factors seem more transportable to other countries. Accordingly, western industrial leaders agitate for legislation to reduce the power of labour and to improve the savings/capital investment climate. Group-think/consensus mechanisms for work improvement are the one factor on the list that may be considered by internal industrial managers for possible implementation in western plants.

Western managerial decision making often relies on individualistic specialist analysis to provide data, followed by the actual decision by executive fiat; a change to the Japanese system of generalist-managers and consensus process *(nemawashi)*[14]

Richard J. Schonberger, "Work Improvement Programmes: Quality Control Circles Compared with Traditional Western Approaches," 3.2 (1983): 18–32.

at the managerial level would be a major upheaval. But Japanese consensus processes involving workers at the shop level of decision analysis are more easily accepted in the west. Quality control circles, a Japanese innovation, circa 1962, that formally mobilises small voluntary worker teams in order to improve quality, productivity, and worker morale, have been a magnet for the attention of western managers. Western corporations initially believed that "it won't work here." But in 1974 a few western companies, led by Lockheed of California, tried quality control circles. The results seemed good, which suggested that there are no particular cultural impediments to the use of QC circles outside of Japan; today numerous western companies have instituted QC circle programmes. (In the United States quality control circles are more often referred to by the shorter term, quality circles.) The quality circle concept is especially popular among training and development officers in industry, as well as organisational behaviourists in the business schools. Quality circles seem to fit well with popular precepts of organisational behaviour: worker participation and group dynamics.

As popular as quality circles have become, a Harvard study group found that Japanese subsidiary plants in North America generally have not implemented circles[16]. This may reflect Japanese caution. Alternatively, circles may be low on the priority list of management tasks to be accomplished. Hayes notes that "most of the (Japanese) plants I visited had . . . experienced problems with QC's for three or four years after their introduction. Moreover, most of the companies I talked to already had enviable reputations for high-quality products by the time they adopted QC's[6]." Furthermore, there is at least some skepticism among the Japanese about the QC wide concept itself. Seiunemo Inaba, president of Fujitsu Fanuc, a premier robot manufacturer, told a group of US visitors, including U.S. senators, that quality control circles are "ritualistic" and unlikely to yield many useful suggestions[10]. QC circles may have only a modest impact, because as Junji Noguchi, general manager of the Union of Japanese Scientists and Engineers, notes, "Workers and foremen can solve only 15 percent of all quality control problems. The rest must be handled by management or the engineering staff[4]."

J. M. Juran, a U.S. authority on quality control who played an important role in helping the Japanese to trigger their "quality revolution," makes the same point, only more emphatically: "There is no possibility for the workforce to make a major contribution to solving a company's quality problems[8]. Juran explains further that QC circles (which he approves of as a human relations tool) can attend to the "trivial many," but major quality problems are beyond the sphere of worker influence—in vendor relations, management policies, process designs, and so forth.

Robert Cole, long an authority on Japanese work cultures, cautions that since "few (American) companies have had the circles in operation more than two years . . . , it would be premature to make assessments as to their suitability to the American environment[3]."

## QC Circles and Similar Programmes _____

The term *quality control circle* is potentially misleading. It suggests that quality control is its orientation, when actually most QC circles are concerned with work improvement in general, not just quality. It is true that many or most QC circles in Japan did initially focus on quality matters only. The QC circle movement appears to date back to 1962 when the journal *Gemba To QC* (Quality Control for Foremen) began publication. Foremen who received the journal formed study groups composed of their own workers in order to share the lore contained in the journal and discuss ways to implement QC concepts[9]. Later the mission of most circles shifted more toward quality problem solving and work improvement in general. Morale benefits have always been implicit inasmuch as worker participation of any kind is thought to improve worker morale.

In each of the many western companies that have adopted a quality control circle programme, there probably were a few doubting Thomas's who viewed the programme as another addition to a long line of work improvement programmes tried by the company over the years. Old-timers may claim that quality circles are "just the same as our old work simplification programme"; some may even assert that circles are the same as their zero defects programme or their employee suggestions programme.

Quality circles are similar to but not the same as work simplification, zero defects, or employee suggestion programmes. Other work improvement programmes that overlap somewhat with quality circles include value engineering/value analysis, industrial engineering/work study, and quality assurance/quality control, each of which exists as a formal organisational unit in many companies.

There may be a basic difference in attitude toward such programmes in the west versus Japan. Western industry tends to build a formal programme, and perhaps a new organisational unit to administer it, each time a promising new management approach appears. The more programmes, the better—is the apparent attitude. Some Japanese firms may have that attitude, but most seem oppositely inclined: The less programmes, and programme organisational units, the better.

Quality control circle programmes are an exception. Many Japanese companies have them. The difference is that the Japanese are not so likely to have numerous other large work improvement programmes that overlap with the QC circle programme. The following discussion of seven related work improvement programmes elaborates upon the point.

## QC Circle Programmes _____

A quality control circle is a small, formally-organised group of workers. The agenda and procedures followed by a QC circle are usually quite structured. The details and the analytical tools vary somewhat from firm to firm, depending upon the objectives that are being emphasised. For example, flow process charts might be used where methods improvement goals are foremost; and fishbone (cause-and-effect) diagrams might be developed to improve quality [7, Ch. 3]. In Japanese QC circles methods and quality objectives are usually given major emphasis, but quality circles in some western companies are not given those objectives. In both western and Japanese circles, morale-enhancing ideas, such as constructing lunch tables or establishing recreation programmes, are legitimate discussion topics, and motivational benefits are an objective which is expected to derive naturally from the employee participation that takes place in circles. Indeed it is common for morale and motivation to be stated as the main objectives of some quality circle programmes, especially in the west.

The next three work improvement programmes are like QC circles in that they involve workers. The programmes are very western, but not very Japanese. Japanese plants with quality control circles already have worker involvement, and why duplicate?

## Western Programmes Featuring Worker Involvement

The western worker involvement-oriented programmes are: zero defects, employee suggestions, and work simplification. Each programme differs from QC circles in one or more key characteristics.

### Zero Defects Programmes

Zero defects (ZD) sounds as if it might extensively duplicate quality control circles. Actually ZD and QC circles are quite different in *modus operandi.* Whereas QC circles involve workers in groups, formal ZD programmes usually involve workers as *individuals* [17, pp. 351–3]. And while QC circles usually follow a formal step-by-step procedure in the process of generating ideas, ZD calls for the worker to perform just one formal step: fill out an "error cause removal" form and turn it in. With regard to objectives, ZD is limited to quality improvement, whereas QC circles seek to improve quality, methods, morale, and motivation.

It could be maintained that since ZD involves workers, there should be derivative motivational advantages. Perhaps so. On the other hand, one could argue that ZD does not result in motivation so much as it *relies on* motivation. ZD seems to have enjoyed particular success in its early years in the U.S. aerospace industry. ZD programmes were launched in the early 1960s when the U.S. was concerned about the "missile gap" with the Soviet Union. Patriotic feelings ran high, and patriotic motivation made it easy for workers to accept a zero defects pledge.

### Employee Suggestion Programmes

Employee suggestion programmes, by numerous names, are very common in western industry but less so in Japan. Suggestions are individually generated, and no formal step-by-step procedures for innovation are followed. Employee suggestion programmes have all of the objectives of QC circles, plus one more: product design improvement. Employee suggestion programmes generally provide for cash awards, which, along with the opportunity to be involved, should result in derivative motivational improvements.

### Work Simplification Programmes

In a work simplification programme, workers and supervisors learn how to conduct systematic methods studies using standard work study aids: process flow charts, man-machine charts, principles of motion economy, and so forth. So trained, the line employees may study and improve their own tasks, rather than being studied by staff analysts from industrial engineering. Work simplification programmes, developed in the United States, were prevalent in U.S. industry in the 1940s in connection with the war production effort. Scarcities of industrial engineers, plus the inherent good sense of studying one's own job, provided rationale for worker involvement in work simplification. Regression has taken it's toll on worker simplification, and only a few programmes still exist. (One example: a longstanding work simplification programme at the Dynamatic Division of Eaton Corporation[15]). But work simplification warrants our consideration since it is the programme most nearly like QC circles. The improvement approaches followed in the two programmes feature the same key characteristics: Worker involvement, group orientation, and procedures. (Both programmes employ step-by-step procedures following the scientific method of inquiry, but specific steps and study aids differ.) The main differences are in objectives. Work simplification is limited to study of work methods, and does not include quality or morale-enhancing improvements.

## Specialist-Based Programmes _____

Worker-oriented QC circles may also be compared with specialist-oriented work improvement programmes. A specialist's job is to introduce special expertise where the situation warrants—or, to use an organisational development term, where "an intervention" is needed.

The obvious deficiencies in a system relying heavily on specialist intervention lead many of us to an intuitive preference for the non-specialist ways of accomplishing the same objectives. That is, we tend to prefer work improvement programmes that aim at getting employees to generate their own improvements rather than being subject to outside intervention. As Ouchi has observed[14], the Japanese are inclined to avoid excessive specialisation and to nurture generalist decision makers with line, rather than staff, responsibilities. Somehow western industry has become rather bogged down with specialists.

There are three specialties considered below that are particularly relevant to this discussion of programmes similar to quality control circles: value engineering/ value analysis, industrial engineering/work study, and quality assurance/quality control.

### Value Engineering/Value Analysis

Value analysis (VA) was developed in the purchasing department of General Electric in 1947[11]. Value analysis means analysing product designs in order to improve value, i.e., cut cost. Value analysis is known as value engineering (VE) in organisations in which the programme responsibility has been assumed by product design engineers. The VA/VE study procedure is formal and systematic; one step in the procedure is an idea-generation method called "brainstorming," which is also one of the steps often followed in QC circle investigations. VA/VE also is similar to quality control circles in that both involve group study. There the similarity ends. VA/VE is a specialist, not a worker function, and the sole objective of VA/VE is product design improvement, which is an objective that is *not* pursued in QC circle programmes. Thus a VA/VE programme might be considered more as complimentary to a QC circle programme than as an alternative.

### Industrial Engineering/Work Study

One function of the industrial engineering profession is to conduct work studies to improve work methods. Some work study procedures and analytical aids, such as process flow charts, are also used by QC circles. In the IE/work study approach, specialists work as individuals, which is contrary to both the worker and the group orientation of QC circles. Work methods improvement, an objective of IE/work study is also one of the QC circle objectives.

### Quality Assurance/Quality Control

The points made about IE/work study also apply to quality assurance/quality control (QA/QC), except that quality rather than work methods is the QA/QC objective: QA/QC shares just one objective (quality), as well as some of the procedures (e.g., statistical quality control charting) with quality control circles; and QA/QC employs specialists working as individuals, whereas QC circles involve employees in groups.

## Quality Control Circles in Perspective ————————————————————————

It is tempting to conclude that quality control circles are a work improvement programme that western industry can do without, inasmuch as most features of QC circle programmes may be covered by other programmes, old and new. A counter argument is that the Japanese seem frequently to be successful *with* QC circles and often *without* most of the other worker-involvement programmes and with *far smaller* specialist-oriented work improvement functions.

Regarding the specialist functions, we know that the Japanese are among the world's leaders in per capita degrees in industrial engineering, and that Japanese training in quality control is unparalleled elsewhere. But in Japanese plants, employees who are educated or trained in industrial engineering and quality control frequently occupy supervisor or other general management positions, rather than being employed only in specialised IE and QC programmes. Juran[8] explains that in Japan most of the "quality-oriented functions are carried out by line personnel. The Japanese do have quality departments, but they are small and perform a limited array of functions. . . ." Japanese industrial engineering functions follow somewhat the same pattern.

A few points seem to emerge from the above discussion of quality control circles and related work improvement programmes:

1. The quality control circle is a recombination of the features of a variety of other work improvement programmes that exist in western industry—and thus is not so unique as is popularly thought.

2. QC circles have contributed to Japanese industrial performance, but perhaps not always in a dominant way.

3. QC circles should be helpful to some western companies in competing with the Japanese, but we might expect the impact of QC circles to vary from case to case, much as has been true of other western work improvement programmes. That is, QC circles could be: (a) as vital as industrial engineering and quality control are for some firms; (b) a modest but sustaining force, perhaps similar to value engineering, in other firms; and (c) a promising programme that fades into disuse—somewhat like work simplification—in still other firms.

4. What is important are the objectives of the seven work improvement programmes that have been discussed: better work methods, quality, product design, morale, and motivation. It is notable that Japanese companies are able to achieve these objectives with less of the formal work improvement programmes that are popular outside of Japan. The ability to achieve those objectives with little fuss and cost is surely the ideal.

In summary, it seems that the best course of action for western manufacturers is to develop simple, low-cost work improvement approaches that fit well with their particular work cultures. The efforts of one Japanese subsidiary operating in the US to do this are examined next.

## Work Improvement Programme at Kawasaki, USA _____

Kawasaki began manufacturing motorcycles in the United States at a plant in Lincoln, Nebraska, in 1975. Most parts for street bikes are fabricated in Japan and shipped in knocked-down (KD) sets of 200 motorcycle equivalents. Exceptions are such major modules as frames and fuel tanks which are fabricated in the Lincoln plant in order to avoid high costs of shipping bulky frames and damage-susceptible tanks.

During 1980, Kawasaki management invested considerable time and money to develop a material requirements planning (MRP) system. MRP was expected to improve the planning of fabricated frames, fuel tanks, and so forth so that delivery of locally-fabricated and purchased parts to the assembly lines would be as reliable as were the deliveries of KD sets from Japan. In early 1981 the MRP project was abandoned in favour of a simpler Japan-style production and work improvement programme. A key thrust of the programme is in altering the physical plant configuration in ways that directly improve productivity and also sharply cut in-process inventories. The inventory-reduction aspect of the programme is called *just-in-time* (JIT) production. Just-in-time production, along with the Japanese *kanban* technique ([12],[13],[17]), have been receiving considerable attention in western industry. The plant configuration aspect of Japanese production systems seems of basic importance but has been generally neglected in published articles thus far. The notion that plant configuration is of central importance seems to have dawned on Kawasaki, Lincoln's, management gradually in the months following the decision to abandon MRP. Finally, early in 1981, Mr. Denis Butt, the American plant manager, issued a formal policy statement reflecting the Kawasaki plant configuration vision.

### Plant Configuration "Vision"

The Kawasaki policy statement is as follows:

*The whole plant is visualised as a series of stations on the assembly lines, whether physically there or not.*

The general idea is to move away from job-lot fabrication and subassembly, and toward repetitive production line operations at every stage of manufacture. The Japanese have become the world's most proficient repetitive manufacturers by following that strategy. By its policy statement, Kawasaki articulated that strategy clearly, in English, and issued it as a top-priority plant objective.

The means of moving toward the plant vision or ideal plant configuration is much different at Kawasaki, Lincoln, than in Japan. In Japanese industry manufacturing engineering is an obsession. One western visitor to Japan, who spent three weeks touring the Toyota family of companies, reports[5] that every supervisor he talked with is or is studying to be an industrial engineer. As these supervisors move upwards in their organisations, the IE or, manufacturing engineering inclinations become pervasive throughout management. In some Japanese plants line workers (perhaps as members of QC circles) also receive training in and the chance to apply manufacturing engineering. This leads to generation of work improvement suggestions throughout the workforce. The best ideas tend to be smoothly implemented after Japanese-style consensus mechanisms *(nemawashi)* have occurred.

The plant-configuration-oriented work improvement programme at Kawasaki, Lincoln, operates without supervisor-engineers and managers steeped in IE concepts, quality circles, and consensus-based decision making. These would be nice to have; indeed, increased use of IE training and consensus mechanisms is probably a worthy long-run objective for western industry, including Kawasaki. In the meantime Kawasaki must get along with what it has: (1) a white collar staff that has gained its experience in the U.S. society and work environment, which features an individualistic specialist-oriented mode of decision analysis and implementation, and (2) a typical U.S. blue color workforce whose high mobility and turnover mitigates against high investment in training workers in the area of work improvement analysis.

### Innovation, Plus Trial-and-Error

The western work environment typically allows white collar employees relatively wide latitude for independent thought. While this may provide fertile ground for generating innovative ideas, the same independent thought processes often result in implementation difficulties. At Kawasaki the overall plant configuration vision is repeatedly emphasised by plant management, to the point where it tends to become instilled in people's thinking, and the apparent effect is that there is a rather high degree of consensus about primary plant objectives. In this sense the overall plant vision may act as a rough surrogate for group consensus mechanisms.

In early 1981 numerous innovative ideas were generated and, in typical U.S. fashion, some were hurriedly and not always thoughtfully tried out. A few were failures. For example, the first attempt at using the kanban parts ordering and delivery system was curtailed as a failure. But the environment discourages people from clinging unreasonably to pet projects, because management has a dominant and agreed upon test of a project's success: Did it or did it not move the plant in the general direction of the repetitive production line mode of operation? In this way the plant vision acts as a quick arbitor on questions of whether to proceed or to stop and try something else.

The ratio of successes to failures is, of course, enhanced by knowledge of what improvement attempts have been successful in Kawasaki's Japanese plants. The knowledge consists not just of unrelated tooling improvements here and there. Rather there seems to be a pattern of physical configuration improvement stages that Japanese manufacturing processes go through in moving toward more streamlined, repetitive manufacturing.

## Plant Configuration Stages _____

Evolution toward a repetitive production line mode of operation is in large measure an attack on large lot sizes, which are commonly associated with job-shop production control. The ideal is repetitive (lotless) production with the capability to run mixed models [17, Ch. 6]. Lotless production is common in the process industries (e.g., refining), because it is natural for many of the products—liquids, gases, flakes, pellets—to flow continuously rather than to be apportioned into lots. In discrete production, repetitive processing is sometimes found in final assembly—occasionally with mixed models, as is common in some farm tractor plants[19]. Since final assembly is generally labour intensive, changing from model to model may involve only a shift from one hand tool and part size to another, as mixed models advance along the line.

In more capital-intensive processes, such as subassembly and fabrication, quick setup or changeover is a greater problem. The machine tools, dies, fixtures and jigs are usually cumbersome to setup. It may take hours to setup for a new model in subassembly and fabrication, as opposed to perhaps seconds to change hand tools on an assembly line. Long setups lead to batching into economic lot sizes, which are comparatively large.

The Japanese are less willing to accept setup time as a given. The Japanese supervisor, imbued with manufacturing engineering training, constantly looks for small modifications to make the jig more versatile and the dies and cutting tools quicker to change.

Setup time reductions open up a host of opportunities to streamline the production system by altering plant configurations. Four distinct plant configuration stages seem to be identifiable in this evolution toward lotless repetitive manufacturing. The configurations themselves are not Japanese, but are universal. The Japanese contribution is their acute appreciation of the benefits of rapidly moving from the less to the more streamlined configurations. The four configurations are:

- Job shop fabrication
- Dedicated production lines

■ Physically-merged production stages
■ Mixed-model processing

Each of these configurations is discussed below, supported by examples from the Kawasaki plant in Nebraska.

### Job-Shop Fabrication

Metal fabrication shops are the classic case of process layouts and production runs based on economic lot sizing. Extensive production control is needed to handle the high inventories, queues, and late orders, and all of the attendant "shop paper," including work orders, dispatch lists, and move tickets. Material requirements planning is an excellent tool for upgrading the production planning and control of fabrication work, and as was noted earlier, Kawasaki plant management initiated and then terminated a project to install MRP.

Now Kawasaki is improving job-shop management not through inventory planning (e.g., MRP) but via a work improvement programme aimed at more-streamlined plant configurations. More specifically, the programme attacks the root of the job-shop "problem," which in the Japanese view is *setup time*.

A notable success is setup time reductions in the punch press work area where motorcycle frame parts are formed from tube stock. There are hundreds of frame pieces to be formed. Setup to make a given part number had been taking several hours, which includes movement of heavy dies into place, numerous adjustments, trials, inspections, more adjustments, and so forth. Today these setups average eight to nine minutes.

The phenomenal setup time reductions were achieved by outfitting the punch presses—about 13 of them—with roller conveyor in a carousel arrangement around the presses at bed height. Figure 1 is a schematic drawing. At the start of each work day the carousel conveyors are loaded with dies arranged in the same order as scheduled production for that day. The operator rotates the proper die into place for each new part number. Quick die change times make it economical to run small lots of many different part numbers per day.

The punch press work area is still a job shop, but the quick passage of very small lots into, through, and out of the presses yields some of the efficiencies of a production line. If, in the future, setup times were to be cut to seconds instead of minutes, it might become feasible to relayout and transform the shop into a true production line, running the same mixture of part numbers as are being used each day in final assembly.

We are talking about a particular shop in a particular company. But the Japanese concept of dealing with job-shop inefficiencies through setup time reductions seems to have generality. The western tendency, or fallacy, is to assume that setup times and large-lot production are a given—to be managed by installing complex computer-based inventory systems.

### Dedicated Production Lines

In another stage of manufacture Kawasaki went beyond setup time reductions to fully convert a job shop to a production line. The shop involved is motorcycle frame

### Figure 1
## PUNCH PRESS EQUIPPED WITH CAROUSEL CONVEYOR FOR QUICK CHANGE OF DIES

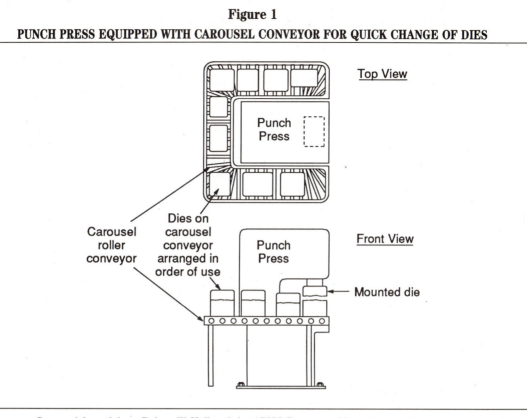

*Source:* Adapted from Robert W. Hall and the APICS Repetitive Manufacturing Group, "Kawasaki U.S.A.; Transferring Japanese Production Methods to the United States: A Case Study," (Washington, D.C.: American Production and Inventory Control Society, 1981).

welding (which follows punch press fabrication of frame parts). The shop had consisted of a number of general-purpose welding booths. A job order to make a lot of given frame model would go to one welder, who would set up welding jigs and weld some of the frame pieces together. The lot then went to a second booth, where another welder set up to weld more pieces to the frame. After several days and several welding booths, the job order would be complete. A good deal of production control was required for scheduling, daily dispatching, work-in-process inventory control, parts movement, and so forth.

In spring 1981, the welders rebuilt their shop into several production lines, each dedicated to a single motorcycle frame model. Tubing may arrive in lots and finished frames may depart in lots. But within welding, production is one frame at a time—lotless, like a bucket brigade. That is, three or four pieces of tubing may be placed in a jig for welding at station one; the assembly is directly passed to station two where more pieces are welded in place using another jig; and on to other stations until the completed frame emerges. The line must be well-balanced (using time study and manipulation of the number of pieces welded at each station) in order to achieve the productivity gains that are the ultimate rationale for a production line.

There are various production control options for the dedicated production line configuration. The option that Kawasaki has implemented, a simple daily schedule, replaces cumbersome order tracking devices—job orders, dispatch lists, move tags, hot lists, and so forth—that are associated with the job-shop configuration.

A second option, which provides tighter inventory control, is to employ kanban instead of a daily schedule. Kanban serves to communicate the need for parts in a using area to a producing area [12]—a "pull" system rather than a pre-scheduled "push" system of ordering. For example, kanban (cards) could be sent from frame painting to the dedicted frame welding lines to trigger an order for more of a given frame part number. Such a use of kanban seems likely as a future development at Kawasaki. (Note: Kawasaki's dedicated welding lines do not operate all the time. Welders are moved from line to line according to the schedule of frame models needed to support the final assembly schedule.)

There is nothing Japanese about a dedicated production line. Rather, the example of Kawasaki's conversion of a job shop to dedicated production lines demonstrates another simple Japanese solution to the job-shop inefficiency problem, for which western industry is more likely to prescribe a complex information system solution.

## Physical Merger of Production Stages

If job shops are converted to production lines, the next stage in streamlining the plant would seem to be to physically merge the separate production lines. The ultimate vision for Kawasaki would be a single grand production line encompassing punch-press forming of frame parts, frame welding, frame painting, and final assembly as the main line. Secondary lines merged with final assembly would provide wheels, gas tanks, engines, small parts, and so forth.

Such a configuration would not even be contemplated in most western companies. At Kawasaki, Lincoln, the plant vision calls for it, and there are several examples, so far, of physically-merged stages. One example is subassembly of differentials for the three-wheeled recreational bike (the "KLT"). Subassembly had been off-line. But in spring, 1981, the KLT supervisor initiated and led a project in which his own assembly line workers moved the differential subassembly facility to the location where differentials are installed in final assembly. (The supervisor was behaving like an IE-trained Japanese supervisor.) There is no longer a separate schedule, inventory, move tickets and so forth for differential production. The KLT assembly schedule covers differentials as well.

A second example of physically merged processes is in wheel mounting. Tires had been mounted on rims off-line and then put onto an overhead conveyor for delivery to the main street bike final assembly line. In autumn 1981, under new plant management (Mr. Ando, a Japanese, replaced Mr. Butt, the American), the conveyor was dismantled, and wheel subassembly physically became a station abutting the point of wheel use on the assembly line. In this case, the subassembly process had previously been physically connected to final assembly, but by a conveyor which cost money, took up space, and held inventory. Eliminating the conveyor tightened control and streamlined the flow.

In the modern Japanese scheme of things, conveyors are necessary as transfer devices in automated production but sometimes frowned upon for their inflexibility in labour-intensive production. The idea is that when you must use human workers, you should take full advantage of human flexibility—to change staffing levels on a given line, for example—and rigid conveyors can get in the way. Conveyors as distance spanners are viewed as undesirable. The Japanese prefer wheeled push racks and dollies, configured to hold a precise, easily counted quantity. In this regard, Mr. Ando, the new plant manager, had a second conveyor dismantled, one that moved gas tanks from tank fabrication to final assembly. Now tanks move on wheeled racks that hold exactly 40 tanks.

These points about conveyors are side issues, but they help reinforce the fundamental message, which is that a plant-configuration-oriented work improvement programme seems considerably more essential in the Japanese production management system than does a quality control circle programme.

### Mixed-Model Processing

A fourth configuration is running mixed models down a single production line instead of separate models down several dedicated lines. Mixed-model processing is a sequencing and scheduling issue as well as a configuration issue. Western writings generally focus on sequencing and line balancing and understate or neglect the configuration issue, which actually may be the major problem in running mixed models. Also western literature generally is limited to discussing mixed models in final *assembly*. A reason is that it is a considerable manufacturing engineering feat to configure multiple *subassembly* or *fabrication* lines to run mixed models, because the equipment—jigs, machine tools, etc.—is not inherently versatile.

For example, for Kawasaki to combine its dedicated frame welding lines into a single mixed-model line would require development of highly versatile jigs and clamping devices capable of holding any size of motorcycle frame. The payoff for doing so would be a great reduction in number of stations, amount of equipment, and floor space, with far higher capacity utilisation. Western manufacturers generally do not even think about mixed models in capital-intensive subassembly and fabrication processes, because of the engineering hurdles. The Japanese will sometimes make the effort.

Labour-intentive final assembly is where both western and Japanese plants are most likely to run mixed models, because people can change from one part and tool to another rather easily as different models flow through. There are some critical configuration hurdles to overcome, however. Kawasaki motorcycle lines in Japan have been running semi-mixed models—five of one model, then five of another, etc.—for several years. By contrast, Kawasaki, Lincoln, had been "stuck" on runs of 200 of a given model between line changes. When Mr. Ando assumed the plant managership, he was determined to reconfigure to achieve the "5–5" model mix that Japan was running. He did better than that. In January, 1982, the Lincoln plant achieved "1–1," or full mixed-model sequencing. The conversion required simple configuration improvements, but a great many of them. For about three months, engineers, material controllers, supervisors, and assemblers worked to build special parts feeder racks, tool holders, colour coding, and precise locations for all assembly racks and implements along the main assembly line. The purpose was to cut line changeover time to the bone. Now, with mixed model assembly, a given worker can quickly adjust to each new model, because parts and tools are in a prescribed easily-accessible place, and there is a distinct colour of part rack and tool (where applicable) that goes with a given motorcycle model.

Western visitors to Japanese plants often comment on the order and discipline they see, and there is a tendency to view it as a cultural trait of Japanese workers. An alternative view is that plant management has invested time, money and effort in developing streamlined plant configurations that remove sources of variability, e.g. uncertain positioning and means of identifying parts, tools and so forth. With a more organised—or disciplined, if you will—task environment, the workers may *seem* to be inherently disciplined.

## Conclusions

In this article I have tried to show that worker involvement is no substitute for good management and engineering, and that both Japanese quality control circles and various western programmes for work improvement and productivity are insufficient as prescriptions for competing with the Japanese. Little has been said about Japanese-style human resource management, inventory management, total quality control, and automation, which are important and significant. Instead I have focused on plant configuration improvements, which is an aspect of Japanese manufacturing management having a far-reaching impact. The subject has been neglected or misunderstood among those of us in the west who are attempting to understand the roots of Japanese productivity. The examples of Kawasaki, Lincoln's rather intensive efforts to streamline and upgrade their plant configuration serve to make the additional point that western managers and workers are capable of operating plants in the high-performance Japanese mode—if they are steered in the right direction.

## References

1. American Production and Inventory Control Society, "Kawasaki USA: Transforming Japanese Production Methods to the United States," a case study prepared by Robert W. Hall, September, 1981.
2. Beach, Dale S., *Personnel: The Management of People at Work,* 2nd ed. New York, Macmillan, 1970.
3. Cole, Robert E., "Learning from the Japanese: Prospects and Pitfalls," *Management Review,* September, 1980, pp 22–8.
4. Gray, Christopher S., "Total Quality Control in Japan—Less Inspection, Lower Cost," *Business Week,* July 16, 1981, pp. 23–35.
5. Hay, Ed., "Planning to Implement Kanban," presentation to APICS Repetitive Manufacturing Group, Just-in-Time Workshop, Lincoln, Nebraska June 11–12, 1981.
6. Hayes, Robert H., "Why Japanese Factories Work," *Harvard Business Review* July-August, 1981, pp. 57–66.

7. Ishikawa, Kaoru, *Guide to Quality Control,* Tokyo: Asian Productivity Organisation, 1972.

8. Juran, J. M., "Product Quality—A Prescription for the West," *Management Review,* Vol. 70, No. 7 July, 1981, pp. 57–61.

9. Kusaba, Ikuro, "Quality Control in Japan," in *Reports of QC Activities,* published by the Union of Japanese Scientists and Engineers, No. 14, 1981, pp. 1–5.

10. Lehner, Urban C., "Oriental Hospitality: Japanese Factories Are Points of Interest to Foreign Tourists Studying Technology," *The Wall Street Journal,* Thursday, September 3, 1981, p. 40.

11. Miles, Lawrence D., *Techniques of Value Analysis and Engineering,* McGraw-Hill, New York, 1961.

12. Monden, Yasuhiro, "Adaptable Kanban System Helps Toyota Maintain Just-in-Time Production," *Industrial Engineering,* May, 1981, p. 29–46.

13. Monden, Yasuhiro, "What Makes the Toyota Production System Really Tick?" *Industrial Engineering,* January, 1981, 36–46.

14. Ouchi, William G., "Theory Z: How American Business Can Meet the Japanese Challenge," Reading, Massachusetts, Addison Wesley, 1981.

15. Repetitive Manufacturing Group of the American Production and Inventory Control Society, "Just-in-Time Workshop," Lincoln, Nebraska, June 11–12, 1981: general discussion of work simplification.

16. Sasser, Earl, "Quality: A Presentation to the A.I.D.S. Group," an unpublished summarisation of materials presented at the national conference of the American Institute for Decision Sciences, Boston: November 18–20, 1981.

17. Schonberger, Richard J., *Japanese Manufacturing Techniques: Nine Hidden Lessons in Simplicity,* The Free Press, New York, 1982 (prepublication copy).

18. Schonberger, Richard J., *Operations Management: Planning and Control of Operations and Operating Resources,* Business Publications, Inc., Dallas, Texas, 1981.

19. Wild, Ray., *Mass-production Management: The Design and Operation of Production Flow-line Systems,* Wiley, London, 1972.

# IV ———— SPECIAL TOPICS ————————————

# 9. THE PRODUCTIVITY PARADOX

## WICKHAM SKINNER

*Wickham Skinner,* James E. Robinson Professor of Business Administration at the Harvard Business School, teaches production and operations management, and has focused recently on the revitalization of U.S. industry. This article, which appeared in the July–August 1986 issue of the *Harvard Business Review,* was accorded the McKinsey Foundation Award as the best article published in the *Harvard Business Review* in 1986, and is reprinted here by special permission. Copyright © 1986 by the President and Fellows of Harvard College. All rights reserved.

The past decade has seen US manufacturers striving to improve productivity and enhance their international competitiveness through a variety of cost-cutting productivity programs. Yet the poor results suggest that the very way managers define productivity and the tools they use to achieve it are pushing their goal further out of reach, the author contends. In this McKinsey Award-winning article he suggests that the best way to achieve lasting improvements is to wean production management from their operational mind-set and involve them in developing strategies that use manufacturing as a competitive tool.

The near-heroic efforts of American manufacturers to regain a competitive edge through productivity improvements have been disappointing. Worse, the results of these efforts have been paradoxical. The harder these companies pursue productivity, the more elusive it becomes.

In the late 1970s, after facing a severe loss of market share in dozens of industries, U.S. producers aggressively mounted programs to revitalize their manufacturing functions. This effort to restore the productivity gains that had regularly been achieved for over 75 years has been extraordinary. (Productivity is defined by the Bureau of Labor Statistics as the value of goods manufactured divided by the amount of labor input. In this article "productivity" is used in the same sense, that is, as a measure of manufacturing employees' performance.) Few companies have failed to measure and analyze productivity or to set about raising output/input ratios. But the results overall have been dismal.

From 1978 through 1982 U.S. manufacturing productivity was essentially flat. Although results during the past three years of business upturn have been somewhat better, they have run 25 percent lower than productivity improvements experienced during earlier, postwar upturns.

## "Boosting" Productivity _____

Consider, for example, the XYZ Corporation, which I visited recently. The company operates a large manufacturing plant where a well-organized productivity program, marshaling its best manufacturing talent, has been under way for three years. Its objective was to boost productivity so as to remove a 30 percent competitive cost disadvantage.

The program has included: appointing a corporate productivity manager; establishing departmental productivity committees; raising the number of industrial engineering professionals by 50 percent; carrying out operation-by-operation analyses to improve efficiency levels, avoid waste and simplify jobs; retraining employees to work "smarter not harder"; streamlining work flow and material movement; replacing out-of-date equipment; retooling operations to cut operator time; tightening standards; installing a computerized production control system; training foremen in work simplification; emphasizing good housekeeping and cleanliness; and installing a computer-based, measured-day work plan, which allows for daily performance reports on every operation, worker and department.

For all this effort—and all the boost it gave to production managers' morale—little good has come of the program. Productivity has crept up by about 7 percent over three years, but profits remain negligible and market share continues to fall. As one executive said, "It's been great finally getting management support and the resources needed to get this plant cleaned up and efficient. But it is extremely discouraging to have worked so hard and, after three years, to be in worse competitive shape than when we started. I don't know how long we can keep trying harder when it doesn't seem to be getting us anywhere."

Unfortunately, XYZ's frustration with a full-out effort that achieves only insignificant competitive results is typical of what has been going on in much of American industry. Why so little competitive return—even a negative return—on so much effort? Is it the high value of the dollar, which cheapens imports? Is the cost gap just too great for us to overcome? Or are we going at the problems in the wrong way? What is going wrong? Why this apparent paradox?

## The Wrong Approach _____

With these questions in mind, I have visited some 25 manufacturing companies during the last two years. Never have I seen so much energetic attention to productivity starting from the top and ricocheting all the way through organizations. This is American hustle and determination at their best. Productivity committees, productivity czars, productivity seminars and productivity campaigns abound.

But the harder these companies work to improve productivity, the less they sharpen the competitive edge that should be improved by better productivity. Elusive gains and vanishing market share point not to a lack of effort but to a central flaw in how that effort is conceived. The very way managers define productivity improvement and the tools they use to achieve it push their goal further out of reach.

Resolutely chipping away at waste and inefficiency—the heart of most productivity programs—is not enough to restore competitive health. Indeed, a focus on cost reductions (that is, on raising labor output while holding the amount of labor constant or, better, reducing it) is proving harmful.

Let me repeat: not only is the productivity approach to manufacturing management not enough (companies cannot cut costs deeply enough to restore competitive vitality); it actually hurts as much as it helps. It is an instinctive response that absorbs managers' minds and diverts them from more effective manufacturing approaches.

Chipping away at productivity . . .

> . . . *is mostly concerned with direct labor efficiency,* although direct labor costs exceed 10 percent of sales in only a few industries. Thus even an immense jump in productivity—say, 20 percent—would not reverse the fortunes of import-damaged industries like autos, consumer electronics, textile machinery, shoes, or textiles.
>
> . . . *focuses excessively on the efficiency of factory workers.* By trying to squeeze out better efficiency from improved attitudes and tighter discipline on a person-by-person and department-by-department basis, the approach detracts attention from the structure of the production system itself.

Production experience regularly observes a "40 40 20" rule. Roughly 40 percent of any manufacturing-based competitive advantage derives from long-term changes in manufacturing structure (decisions, for example, concerning the number, size, location and capacity of facilities) and basic approaches in materials and work force management. Another 40 percent comes from major changes in equipment and process technology. The final 20 percent—no more—rests on conventional approaches to productivity improvement.

What this rule says is that the least powerful way to bolster competitive advantage is to focus on conventional productivity and cost-cutting approaches. Far more powerful are changes in manufacturing structure and technology. The rule does not, of course, say "Don't try to improve productivity." These well-known tools are easy to use and do help to remove unnecessary fat. But they quickly reach the limits of what they can contribute. Productivity is the wrong tree to bark up.

> . . . *ignores other ways to compete that use manufacturing as a strategic resource.* Quality, reliable delivery, short lead times, customer service, rapid product introduction, flexible capacity and efficient capital deployment—these, not cost reduction, are the primary operational sources of advantage in today's competitive environment.
>
> . . . *fails to provide or support a coherent manufacturing strategy.* By assuming that manufacturing's essential task is to make a company the low-cost producer in its industry, this approach rashly rules out other strategies.

## Flawed Logic

Most of the productivity-focused programs I have seen blithely assume that competitive position lost on grounds of higher cost is best recovered by installing cost-reduction programs. This logic is tempting but wrong. These programs cannot succeed. They have the wrong targets and misconstrue the nature of the competitive challenge they are supposed to address. Worse, they incur huge opportunity costs. By tying managers at all levels to short-term considerations, they short-circuit the development of an aggressive manufacturing strategy.

But they also do harm. These programs can, for example, hinder innovation. As William Abernathy and Kenneth Wayne's study of auto manufacturers has shown, an industry can easily become the prisoner of its own massive investments in low-cost production and in the organizational systems that support it.* When process costs and constraints drive both product and corporate strategy, flexibility gets lost, as does the ability to rapidly introduce product changes or develop new products.

Even more is at stake than getting locked into the wrong equipment. Managers under relentless pressure to maximize productivity resist innovation. Preoccupied as they are with this week's cost performance, they know well that changes in processes or systems will wreak havoc with the results on which they are measured. Consequently, innovations that lead to, say, better service or shorter lead times for product changeovers are certain to suffer.

Innovation is not, however, all that suffers. A full-out concentration on productivity frequently creates an environment that alienates the work force. Pressure for output and efficiency are the staples of factory life as hourly workers experience it. Engineers and supervisors tell them what to do, how to do it, and how long they may take. Theirs is an often unhappy, quota-measured culture—and has been for more than 150 years. In such an environment, even the most reasonable requests are resented.

Recent admirers of the Japanese argue that low cost and high quality can go hand in hand. Indeed, in the right setting managers need not trade one for the other. But in an efficiency-driven operation this logic can be a trap. When low cost is the goal, quality very often gets lost. But when quality is the goal, lower costs do usually follow.

## Operational Mind-Set

The will to make large investments in radically new process technology gets lost, too. The slow adoption of such manufacturing technologies as CAD/CAM, robotics and flexible machining centers reflects managers' wise assumptions that these investments would initially drive productivity down.

Fears that several years of debugging and learning to use the new gear would hurt productivity have already cost many companies valuable time in mastering these process technologies. Even more troubling, the companies have failed to acquire a strategic resource that could help them restore their competitive position. A productivity focus inevitably forces managers into a short-term, operational mind-set. When productivity is driving, experimentation takes a back seat.

*William J. Abernathy and Kenneth Wayne, "Limits of the Learning Curve," *Harvard Business Review,* September–October 1974, p. 109.

The emphasis on direct costs, which attends the productivity focus, leads a company to use management controls that focus on the wrong targets. Inevitably, these controls key on direct labor: overhead is allocated by direct labor; variances from standards are calculated from direct labor. Performance in customer service, delivery, lead times, quality and asset turns are secondary. The reward system based on such controls drives behavior toward simplistic goals that represent only a small fraction of total costs while the real costs lie in overhead and purchased materials.

Why has this gone on year after year even as the cost mix has steadily moved away from direct labor? By now our accounting and control systems are pathetically old-fashioned and ineffective. But nothing changes. Our continuing obsession with productivity as the be-all measure of factory performance is to blame, not the stubbornness of accountants.

## Stunted Vision

When managers grow up in this atmosphere, their skills and vision never fully develop. They instinctively seize on inefficiencies and waste while missing broad opportunities to compete through manufacturing. The harsh fact is that generations of production managers have been stunted by this efficiency-driven mentality. Theirs is the oldest management function, yet today it is often the most backward. Unable to join finance, marketing and general management in thinking strategically about their businesses, they are cut off from corporate leadership. As my recent study of 66 "comers" in production management shows, 10 or 15 years' immersion in a productivity-directed organization creates severe limitations of vision.* In time, these limitations form a long-term mind-set that only a few can shake. Today the production function is seldom the place to find managers who can design competitive manufacturing structures.

Indeed, ever since Frederick Winslow Taylor, our obsession with productivity and efficiency has spoiled the atmosphere of the factory. "Factory" is a bad word. Production managers first came into existence not as architects of competitive systems but as custodians of large, capital-intensive assets. Their job was to control and coordinate all factors of production so as to minimize costs and maximize output. This single dimension of performance is deeply ingrained in production and until recently has sufficed as a basis of evaluation.

Not surprisingly, it created a negative, penny-pinching, mechanistic culture in most factories—a culture that has driven out and kept away creative people at all levels. Who among our young today wishes to work in an environment where one is told what to do, how to do it, when to do it, is measured in minutes and sometimes seconds, is supervised closely to prevent any inefficiencies, and is paced by assembly lines or machines to produce at a rapid and relentless pace?

*Wickham Skinner, "The Taming of Lions: How Manufacturing Leadership Evolved, 1780–1984" in *The Uneasy Alliance,* ed. Kim B. Clark, Robert H. Hayes and Christopher Lorenz, Boston, Harvard Business School Press, 1985, p. 63.

Today's problems in making the factory into a more attractive place to work are not new. They are the direct outcome of the 150-year history of an institution based on productivity. As long as cost and efficiency are the primary measurements of success, the manufacturing plant will continue to repel many able, creative people.

## Breaking Out

Faced with this paradox—efforts to improve productivity driving competitive success further out of reach—a number of companies have broken out of the bind with extraordinary success. Their experience suggests, however, that breaking loose from so long-established a mind-set is not easy. It requires a change in culture, habits, instincts, and ways of thinking and reasoning. And it means modifying a set of values that current reward systems and day-to-day operational demands reinforce. This is a tall order.

Every company I know that has freed itself from the paradox has done so, in part, by:

*Recognizing that its approach to productivity was not working well enough to make the company cost competitive.* This recognition allowed managers to seek strategic objectives for manufacturing other than those determined primarily by cost.

About twelve years ago, a key division of American Standard adopted a "become the low-cost producer" strategy. Its productivity-driven focus did little to reduce costs but had an immediate negative effect on quality, delivery and market share. What Standard needed was a totally new manufacturing strategy—one that allowed different areas of the factory to specialize in different markets and quality levels. When this approach replaced the low-cost strategy, the division regained its strong competitive position within three years.

*Accepting the fact that its manufacturing was in trouble and needed to be run differently.* In the mid-1970s officers of the Copeland Corporation, a large producer of refrigeration compressors, decided that their industry was fast becoming mature. An analysis of their nearly obsolete production facilities and equipment made it clear that manufacturing had become a corporate millstone. Without a major change in the number, size, location and focus of these facilities, long-term survival would be impossible. Copeland made these changes. The results: order-of-magnitude improvements in quality, shortened delivery cycles, lower inventory investments, and much greater flexibility in product and volume changes.

### MANUFACTURING STRATEGY

A manufacturing strategy describes the competitive leverage required of—and made possible by—the production function. It analyzes the entire manufacturing function relative to its ability to provide such leverage, on which task it then focuses each element of manufacturing structure. It also allows the *structure* to be managed, not just the short-term, operational details of cost, quality and delivery. And it spells out an internally consistent set of structural decisions designed to forge manufacturing into a strategic weapon. These structural decisions include:

- What to make and what to buy.
- The capacity levels to be provided.
- The number and sizes of plants.
- The location of plants.
- Choices of equipment and process technology.
- The production and inventory control systems.
- The quality control system.
- The cost and other informat on systems.
- Work force management policies.
- Organizational structure.

*Developing and implementing a manufacturing strategy* (see ruled insert). When production managers actively seek to understand (and, in some cases, to help develop) the competitive strategy of relevant business units, they are better able to work out the objectives for their own function that will turn it into a competitive weapon. The requirements of such a manufacturing strategy will then determine needed changes in the manufacturing system's structure and infrastructure.

*Adopting new process technology.* Changes in equipment and process technology are powerful engines of change. Bringing such technology on line helps force adjustments in work flow, key skills and information systems as well as in systems for inventory control, materials management and human resource management. There are few more effective means of loosening up old ways of organizing production. General Electric and Deere & Company have made wholesale process changes at their dishwasher and locomotive (GE) and tractor (Deere) plants—changes that boosted product quality and reliability. Timken and Cooper Industries have each made large investments in radical new technologies that speeded up their ability to deliver new products and customer specials.

*Making major changes in the selection, development, assignments, and reward systems for manufacturing managers.* The successful companies I looked at decided they needed a new breed of production leader—managers able to focus on a wider set of objectives than efficiency and cost. It was, however, no simple matter to find or train this new breed. Some, in fact, turned up in unexpected places: marketing, sales, engineering, research, general management. As a group, they were good team builders and problem solvers and had broad enough experience to hold their own in top corporate councils. Their companies considered them among the most promising, high-potential "comers" for future leadership at the highest levels.

## A Strategic Role _____

Only when manufacturers were willing to try such novel approaches to the competitive challenges facing them have they broken loose from the productivity paradox and transformed their production function into a strategic weapon. There is hope for manufacturing in America, but it rests on a different way of managing in this oldest of managerial professions.

As we have seen, our pursuit of productivity is paradoxical: the more we pursue it, the more elusive it becomes. An obsession with cost reduction produces a narrowness of vision and an organizational backlash that work against its underlying purpose. To boost productivity in its fullest sense—that is, to unleash a powerful team of people supported by the right technology—we must first let go of old-fashioned productivity as a primary goal. In its place we must set a new, simple but powerful objective for manufacturing: to be competitive.

# 10. COMPARATIVE ANALYSIS OF JAPANESE JUST-IN-TIME PURCHASING AND TRADITIONAL U.S. PURCHASING SYSTEMS

## SANG M. LEE AND A. ANSARI

*University of Nebraska, Lincoln, Nebraska, USA and Albers School of Business, Seattle University, Seattle, Washington, USA respectively*

Received August 1985
Revised September 1985

Just-In-Time (JIT) purchasing has received an increasing amount of attention in the operations management literature. Today, a growing number of U.S. firms have switched to the Japanese JIT purchasing concept in an effort to improve their product quality and productivity. This article discusses the major activities of JIT purchasing and provides a comparative analysis of differences between the JIT purchasing and traditional U.S. purchasing systems. Furthermore, the reasons behind these major differences and their future implications for U.S. firms are discussed.

## Introduction

In the early 1950s, a unique production system emerged in Japanese manufacturing companies which contributed substantially to Japan's high product quality and productivity. During the past two decades, Japan's annual productivity increase rate in manufacturing was 9.3 per cent as compared with 2.7 per cent increase in the U.S. This distinctive Japanese system is widely known as Just-In-Time (JIT) production. An important aspect of JIT that has had a great influence on product quality and productivity is JIT purchasing.

JIT purchasing is an important element of this unique Japanese production planning and inventory control technique. JIT purchasing is effective for the following:

1. controlling the inventory system;
2. reducing buffer inventories;
3. reducing space needed;
4. reducing material handling; and
5. reducing wasted materials.

During the past several years, practitioners and academics who were concerned with product quality and productivity in the United States have focused increasing

Sang M. Lee and A. Ansari, "Comparative Analysis of Japanese Just-In-Time Purchasing and Traditional U.S. Purchasing Systems," *International Journal of Operations and Production Management* 5.4 (1985) 5–14. © 1986 by MCB University Press Limited: all rights reserved.

attention on the potential benefits of the JIT concept. Since the early 1980s, many American and Japanese executives and scholars have participated in regional, national, and international conferences to exchange views on business, economic, and technological advances. One of the most popular topics at these conferences has been the implementation of Japanese manufacturing techniques.

Today, a growing number of U.S. companies has switched to JIT purchasing from traditional U.S. purchasing practices. A few of these companies have implemented their own versions of JIT under different names, such as ZIPS (Zero Inventory Product System), MAN (Material-as-Needed), and Nick-of-Time. By any of these names, JIT treats purchasing the same way[1]: materials are purchased in small quantities with frequent deliveries from a fewer number of close suppliers, just in time for use. It appears certain that during the next few years there will be an accelerated level of interest among many U.S. companies in the implementation of the JIT purchasing concept.

Through interpreting data collected during a recent study this article seeks to:

1. Identify the major activities involved in JIT purchasing.
2. Compare these activities with traditional U.S. purchasing.
3. Discover the reasons behind the differences.
4. Discuss future implications for U.S. firms.

Data collection involved three approaches: questionnaire responses, interviews and collected documents. The first utilised a questionnaire to collect the data in seven categories: company descriptions, transportation/traffic details, vendor relations, quality inspection, benefits of JIT purchasing, implementation problems, and prerequisite variables required for successful implementation.

The second approach consisted of interviews with the purchasing manager, production manager, quality control manager, engineering and design people, and the transportation/traffic manager in four U.S. companies: (1) General Motors Corporation (Buick Division); (2) Hewlett Packard Company (Greeley Division); (3) Nissan Motor Manufacturing Corporation USA (Smyrna plant); and (4) Kawasaki Motors Corporation USA (Lincoln plant). This provided empirical on-site data.

The third method of data collection utilised documents collected from companies and professional associations which are proponents of the JIT effort in the U.S., e.g., Automotive Industry Action Group. The documents collected were used to support management responses from the interviews as well as the responses to the questionnaire.

## JIT Purchasing versus Traditional U.S. Purchasing _____

Purchasing activities include all of the functions involved in the procurement of material, from the time of need to receipt and use of the material. These activities vary considerably among organisations depending on the size of the company. Generally, there are several major activities over which purchasing should have full responsibility, regardless of the organisation's size.

The major activities of purchasing practice are as follows:

1. Determining the purchase lot size
2. Selecting suppliers
3. Evaluating suppliers
4. Receiving inspection
5. Negotiating and bidding process
6. Determining mode of transportation
7. Determining product specification
8. Paperwork
9. Packaging

All of these activities in traditional U.S. purchasing are approached differently from JIT purchasing practices. Table 1 is a summary comparing activities under both systems. Activities are elaborated below.

## Purchase Lot Size

Traditional U.S. purchasing practices generally rely heavily on a just-in-case system. Large batches are purchased based on a delivery schedule specified in the purchase order. This practice allows the company to continue to operate even if there are serious disruptions of supplies[2]. On the other hand, under Japanese JIT purchasing practice the emphasis is placed on the purchase of minimum lot sizes, preferably piece for piece. Piece for piece delivery allows a tighter inventory control which eliminates large stocks of parts between process stages[3, 4].

One of the most important justifications for the traditional purchasing practice of buying in large quantities with less frequent deliveries rather than in small quantities with more frequent deliveries is the realisation of lower shipping and handling costs. Schonberger[4], however, argues that most U.S. companies purchase in large lot sizes because they consider the shipping and handling costs as given items. Under JIT purchasing concept, obtaining small lot sizes is considered a challenge in spite of obstacles such as shipping costs.

There are two approaches[5] which have been used by many U.S. companies, such as Kawasaki (Lincoln Plant), Hewlett-Packard (Greeley, Colorado Division), and General Motors (Buick Division), to reduce JIT shipping costs associated with the frequency of delivery. The first approach is to develop a freight consolidation programme with various suppliers. One of the important benefits of this programme is to aid the suppliers to share delivery trucks. In this arrangement, it is not uncommon to see trucks carrying small quantities of parts from three or four suppliers. Each truck is assigned a time when it can enter the plant and drive directly to the assembly line. The second approach is to select local suppliers, wherever possible. When there is no local source, potential suppliers are encouraged to move their operations close to their plants through offers of long-term contracts.

## Selecting Supplier

The most important activity of purchasing is supplier selection. A key feature of JIT purchasing practices, which differs from traditional U.S. purchasing practices, is the

**Table 1.**

## COMPARATIVE ANALYSIS OF PURCHASING PRACTICE: TRADITIONAL U.S. AND JAPANESE JIT

| Purchasing Activity | JIT Purchasing | Traditional Purchasing |
|---|---|---|
| Purchase Lot Size | Purchase in small lots with frequent deliveries | Purchase in large batch size with less frequent deliveries |
| Selecting Supplier | Single source of supply for a given part in nearby geographical area with a long-term contract | Rely on multiple sources of supply for a given part and short-term contracts |
| Evaluating Supplier | Emphasis is placed on product quality, delivery performance, and price, but *no* percentage of reject from supplier is acceptable | Emphasis is placed on product quality, delivery performance and price but about two per cent reject from supplier is acceptable |
| Receiving Inspection | Counting and receiving inspection of incoming parts is reduced and eventually eliminated | Buyer is responsible for receiving, counting, and inspecting all incoming parts |
| Negotiating and Bidding Process | Primary objective is to achieve product quality through a long-term contract and fair price | Primary objective is to get the lowest possible price |
| Determining Mode of Transportation | Concern for both inbound and outbound freight, and on-time delivery. Delivery schedule left to the buyer | Concern for outbound freight and lower outbound costs. Delivery schedule left to the supplier |
| Product Specification | "Loose" specifications. The buyer relies more on performance specifications than on product design and the supplier is encouraged to be more innovative | "Rigid" specifications. The buyer relies more on design specifications than on product performance and suppliers have less freedom in design specifications |
| Paperwork | Less formal paperwork. Delivery time and quantity level can be changed by telephone calls | Requires great deal of time and formal paperwork. Changes in delivery date and quantity require purchase orders |
| Packaging | Small standard containers used to hold exact quantity and to specify the precise specifications | Regular packaging for every part type and part number with no clear specifications on product content. |

idea of dealing with a small number of nearby suppliers—ideally single sources of supply. Under JIT purchasing, the buyer is encouraged to buy a given part from a single supplier in a nearby geographical area and to establish good long-term relationships with the supplier. Edward Hennessy, CEO at Allied Corporation, argues that:

*Purchasing must cultivate sound relationships with its suppliers so inventories may be reduced to minimum practical levels and quality of supply may be such that rejection of material is essentially eliminated[6].*

Single sourcing is contrary to the typical U.S. purchasing practice which generally relies on multiple sources of supply for a given part. Deere and Company indicated that a few years ago it had many suppliers for a given part and had to split the order among them. For example, they purchased forgings from 50 different companies[7].

Strong arguments arise between those who advocate single sourcing and those who support multiple sourcing. The proponents of multiple sourcing argue that multiple sources of supply give broader advantages to the buyer, such as:

1. It provides a broader technical base to the buyer.
2. It protects the buyer in times of shortages against failure at the supplier's plant.
3. It encourages competition among suppliers in securing the best possible price and products[8].

On the other hand, those U.S. companies that have implemented the JIT purchasing concept realised that having a smaller number of sources of supply results in certain benefits:

1. Consistent quality—involving suppliers in the early stages of product design can consistently provide high quality products.
2. Saving of resources—minimum investment and resources, such as buyer's time, travel, and engineering that are required when there is a limited number of suppliers.
3. Lower costs—the overall volume of items purchased is higher, which eventually leads to lower costs.
4. Special attention—the suppliers are more inclined to pay special attention to the buyer's needs since the buyer represents a large account.
5. Saving on tooling—total dollars spent to provide tooling to the suppliers is minimal since the buyer concentrates on one source of supply.
6. The most important benefit obtained from single sourcing is the establishment of long-term relationships with suppliers, which encourages loyalty and reduces the risk of an interrupted supply of parts to the buyer plant.

## Evaluating Supplier

The evaluation of sources of supply is the most important continuing process of purchasing. Evaluation varies according to the nature, complexity, competition, and dollar value of items purchased. Under traditional U.S. purchasing practices, evaluation is based on three important criteria[9]: product quality, delivery performance and price. Determining which of these factors is the most critical depends on how their relative importance is perceived. A study conducted among 273 purchasing managers[10] listed 23 factors that were considered in evaluating a potential supplier.

This study revealed that product quality and delivery performance were extremely important factors and price was considered merely as an important factor.

One effective method available in evaluating a supplier's quality of performance is to make monthly or quarterly tabulations of the percentage of rejected materials. Another method for rating a supplier's quality performance involves a regularly scheduled review of quality performance among the buyer, suppliers, and the engineering people[8].

Delivery performance includes responses to enquiries, special services rendered, and other intangibles. It is common for U.S. companies to develop a vendor delivery rating scheme that consists of categories, such as top rating, good, fair, and unsatisfactory. The supplier's delivery performance is then tabulated and rated monthly.

Although traditional U.S. purchasing practices and Japanese JIT purchasing practices both emphasize the importance of product quality and delivery performance, emphasis placed on these factors varies between the two approaches. For example, in contrast to the traditional U.S. purchasing practice, where many companies accept about two per cent rejects from suppliers, Japanese JIT purchasing permits no such percentage of rejects because the supplier has the responsibility to deliver just the right number of items. When Hewlett-Packard recently asked for a large sample of a component part, it subjected its potential suppliers to intense reliability testing. The best Japanese supplier had 0.003 per cent unreliability whereas the best American supplier achieved 1.8 per cent unreliability[11].

### Receiving Inspection

Under traditional U.S. purchasing practice, the receiving department is responsible for receipt, identification, piece-by-piece counts and inspection of all inbound freight for quality in accordance with their product design specifications. The responsibility of inspecting the incoming products is almost invariably placed on the buyer. In the Japanese system, receiving inspection is avoided except for new parts and new suppliers[12].

Under JIT purchasing, in most Japanese plants, it is common for suppliers to drive their trucks straight to the assembly line (except for new parts and new suppliers)[13]. This practice is primarily achieved by extending the inspection function of quality back to the supplier's plant and making sure that quality is built-in before the part leaves the supplier's plant.

Many U.S. companies are in the process of moving the responsibility for quality of all incoming parts back to the suppliers. This concept has already been adopted by Nissan (Smyrna plant), GM (Buick Division), Kawasaki (Lincoln plant), and Hewlett-Packard (HP) for some of their potential JIT suppliers. For example, ComMents (CMT), one of HP's suppliers, move their delivery cart directly to the production area without going through inspection, avoiding excessive paperwork, etc[6].

### Negotiating and Bidding Process

Another difference between traditional U.S. and JIT purchasing practices is the negotiating and bidding process. Since the typical U.S. buyer preference is to deal with multiple sources of supply, the traditional bidding process implies that the lowest bid customarily will get the contract. In fact, the main objective in bidding from various sources is to obtain the lowest possible price. The primary reason for this is that most U.S. buyers provide very exact and rigid product specifications for prospective suppliers, and the buying decision is therefore usually based on lowest cost. An important aspect of negotiating contracts is that the supplier offers very short-term contracts and they may be terminated for reasons of competitive price.

In contrast, the objective of bidding under JIT purchasing practices is not just to negotiate for the lowest bid possible, but also to establish a close relationship with the suppliers for the following reasons:

1. The concept of JIT purchasing emphasises a single source of supply. There-fore, the buyer and supplier will agree upon a "fair" price to both parties.
2. The bidding specifications are not as rigid, and suppliers are encouraged to be innovative in meeting the specified needs.
3. Emphasis on product quality is the primary factor in the bidding and negotiation process.
4. An increase in the number of longer term contracts with the possibility of annual negotiation with the supplier, leading to better quality and possible cost reduction.

### Determining Mode of Transportation

Transportation is an important issue in most manufacturing firms. Due to complex-ities involved in transportation, responsibility is often placed in a separate department designated as the traffic department. The responsibilities of the traffic department include outgoing freight and internal plant transportation.

In traditional U.S. manufacturing buying, the handling of inbound freight differs from JIT buying. According to U.S. practice, the primary responsibilities for sched-uling and delivery are generally left to the supplier and the transportation company, regardless of whether the purchase contract states FOB destination or FOB shipping point. The emphasis for U.S. manufacturing traffic managers is therefore on outbound freight. The reasons why many traffic departments do not concentrate on inbound freight is that most industrial traffic departments are measured on how successful they are in lowering outbound transportation costs.

Under JIT buying, the traffic manager is responsible for both inbound and out-bound freight. Schonberger[4] states that:

> JIT buying can hardly be successful if inbound freight scheduling is left to the transportation system, whose primary concern is with optimal utilisation of drivers, storage space, and trailer or rail-car cubes.

Under JIT, traffic managers are more concerned with on-time delivery than with trying to lower outbound costs. They also try to prevent production disruptions in the buyer's plant due to late arrival of goods.

### Product Specification

According to traditional U.S. purchasing practice, the engineering department spec-ifies and develops the tolerance for almost every conceivable design feature of the end product[14]. At the same time, purchasing reviews purchase requirements to make sure that any necessary product specifications (specs) are defined. Suppliers know exactly what the buyer wants[15]. Several types of specs commonly used in the United States are blueprints, performance specs, material specs, etc. The buyers rely more on design specs (which describe and identify the composition of materials to be used, their size, shape, and method of manufacture), than on performance specs. Although the design engineers are responsible for developing these specs, they rarely interact with suppliers. Procurement problems are left to the purchasing department. This reduces the feedback that design engineers will receive from suppliers in the area of design or quality.

Under the JIT purchasing practice, the buyer seeks more technical advice and assistance from suppliers in order to design better parts, achieve lower prices and improve product quality and productivity. The buyer relies more on supplier performance specs and less on narrowly defined design specs. This allows the supplier to use more discretion in making recommendations and innovations when discussing with the buyer any problems with respect to design and quality. Generally, relying on performance specs places greater responsibility on the supplier for satisfactory products. Additionally, work delays are avoided in the supplier's plant because there is more freedom in dealing with product design[4].

## Paperwork

Under traditional U.S. purchasing practice, purchase orders are issued for nearly all requirements such as purchase requisitions, packing lists, shipping documents, invoices, etc. These activities and their supporting documents require a massive amount of time and formal paperwork. Janson[16] explained that in traditional purchasing the paperwork is so extensive that purchasing people spend most of their time pushing paper. Wight suggested that frequent changes in order quantity and delivery times forced purchasing people toward a reactionary "fire-fighting" mode; more than 50 per cent of their time was spent on paperwork and expediting. This gave purchasing people less opportunity to "problem-solve" with suppliers and to work closely together to improve cost efficiency, product design specs, and productivity[17].

JIT purchasing requires much less formal paperwork since: deliveries are made several times a day; long-term contracts are used; and a simple phone call can easily change the delivery timing and quantity level. Also, paperwork is reduced under JIT system by use of Kanban cards which trigger the deliveries. Therefore, purchasing has more time available to spend with the suppliers to improve the product design specs, quality and productivity. For example, Berry[18] explained that Newman Foundries uses its own trucks to deliver aluminum castings to Chevrolet transmission once or twice a day. Newman "may be one of the first suppliers to deliver to GM without paper documentation."

## Packaging

A factor which is often overlooked in traditional U.S. purchasing practices, but with which the buyer should be concerned, is packaging specification and handling. Better packaging and precise specifications of product content not only reduce manpower requirements, but also affect the distributor, retailer, marketing department, and transportation department[15]. Ammer[19] suggested that purchasing should be concerned not only with the flow of materials into the plant and finished products out of the plant, but also with product specification and handling, which might be quite complex and costly.

Aljian[9] indicated that:

> *Packaging improvements may consist of such a small thing as specifying smaller containers to permit one-man handling or to prevent losses due to opened, partially emptied containers which permit loss, deterioration, or contamination.*

Under JIT purchasing the idea is to use small standard containers for every part type and part number. Since the containers hold a precise quantity, the following advantages are realised:

1. No overage/underage allowed.
2. Precise specification of parts on the containers prevents the buyer from making mistakes.
3. It allows easy and accurate count of parts.

MacCallum[20] explained that Honda's suppliers in Japan often use plastic bins to deliver the parts directly to the assembly line. John Stalk, Materials Operations Manager at Xerox[21], explained that under their new programme, Xerox aims to eliminate defective parts through several factors. One of the important factors is better packaging and handling which should arise from a close relationship with suppliers.

## Implications for U.S. Firms _____

The contrast between Japanese purchasing practices and U.S. traditional purchasing practices provides a good insight into the relative importance of JIT for U.S. firms. Japanese automobiles, television sets, cameras, robotics, ceramics, optics, and other products have captured a sizeable portion of the U.S. market. Many authors believe that Japan's success in achieving a high rate of product quality and productivity is largely a result of its manufacturing techniques, especially the JIT system.

Since the initial implementation of JIT purchasing in late 1980 by Kawasaki Motors (Lincoln plant), at least 50 companies in the U.S. such as GM, Ford, Nissan, Hewlett-Packard, Xerox, Goodyear, GE, and other large U.S. corporations, have adopted and implemented the concept in their plants. The implementation of the JIT purchasing concept has significantly altered not only the way these companies plan and control their production facilities and purchasing systems but has also led to improvements in their product quality and productivity[5].

The major activities of JIT purchasing which substantially vary from traditional U.S. purchasing are:

1. *Purchase lot size*—materials are purchased in very small quantities with frequent deliveries;
2. *Selecting supplier*—single sourcing and long-term contract;
3. *Evaluating supplier*—emphasis on quality with no percentage of reject acceptable;
4. *Receiving inspection*—the need for incoming inspection can be reduced;
5. *Negotiating and bidding process*—high quality and fair price;
6. *Transportation*—delivery schedule (inbound and outbound freight) left up to buyer;
7. *Product specs*—use of less rigid material specs and encourage more innovation on the supplier's part;
8. *Paperwork*—eliminate unnecessary paperwork;
9. *Packaging*—utilise small standard containers to hold exact quantity.

## References

1. Waters, C. R., "Why Everybody's Talking About 'Just-In-Time' ", *INC,* Vol. 6 No. 3, March 1984, pp. 77–90.
2. Nellemann, D. O. and Smith, L. F., " 'Just-In-Time' vs. Just-In-Case Production/ Inventory Systems: Concepts Borrowed Back from Japan", *Production and Inventory Management,* Vol. 23 No. 2, Second Quarter, 1982, pp. 12–20.
3. McElroy, J., "Making Just-In-Time Production Pay Off", *Automotive Industries,* Vol. 162 No. 2, February 1982, pp. 77–80.
4. Schonberger, R. J., *Japanese Manufacturing Techniques: Nine Hidden Lessons in Simplicity,* The Free Press, New York, 1982.
5. Ansari, A., "An Empirical Examination of the Implementation of Japanese Just-In-Time Purchasing Practices and Its Impact on Product Quality and Productivity in U.S. Firms", unpublished dissertation, University of Nebraska-Lincoln, 1984.
6. "Secrets of Japanese Success", *Management Today,* January 1981, pp. 64–8.
7. "New Thoughts on Purchasing", *Implement and Tractor,* October 1982, pp. ME-7–ME-22.
8. Lee, L. Jr. and Dobler, D. W., *Purchasing and Materials Management,* third edition, McGraw-Hill Book Company, New York, 1977.
9. Aljian, G. W., *Purchasing Handbook,* third edition, McGraw-Hill Book Company, New York, 1973.
10. Dickson, G. W., "An Analysis of Vendor Selection Systems and Decisions", *Journal of Purchasing,* Vol. 2 No. 1, 1966, pp. 5–17.
11. Tregoe, B. B., "Productivity in America: Where It Went and How to Get It Back", *Management Review,* Vol. 72 No. 2, February 1983, pp. 23–45.
12. Schonberger, R. J. and Ansari, A., " 'Just-In-Time' Purchasing Can Improve Quality", *Journal of Purchasing and Materials Management,* Vol. 20 No. 1, Spring 1984, pp. 2–7.
13. Hartley, J. R., "The World's Greatest Production Line: The Japanese View", *Automotive Industries,* vol. 161 No. 12, December 1981, pp. 53–4.

14. Schonberger, R. J. and Gilbert P. J., "Just-In-Time Purchasing: A Challenge for U.S. Industry", *California Management Review,* Vol. 26 No. 1, Fall 1983, pp. 54–68.

15. Tersine, R. J., *Production/Operations Management: Concepts, Structure, and Analysis,* Elsevier North Holland, Inc., New York, 1980.

16. Janson, R. L., *Purchasing Agent's Desk Book,* Prentice-Hall Inc., Englewood Cliffs, New Jersey, 1980.

17. Morgan, J. P., "MRP Breaks with Past Patterns of Failure", *Purchasing,* Vol. 89 No. 2, 24 July 1980, pp. 48–54.

18. Berry, B. H., "Detroit Automakers Slim Down Inventory to Beef Up Profits", *Iron Age,* Vol. 225 No. 24, 1982, pp. 61–5.

19. Ammer, D. S., *Materials Management and Purchasing,* Richard D. Irwin, Inc., Homewood, Illinois, 1980.

20. MacCallum, F., *Japanese Production Methods and Strategies,* G. M. of Canada, G. M. St. Catherines, 1982.

21. "Quality Rests on an Active Supplier", *Purchasing,* Vol. 92 No. 2, 28 January 1982, pp. 97–100.

# 11. AMERICA'S VERTICAL CUTBACK

## JOHN THACKRAY

*John Thackray* is the U.S. correspondent of the British business monthly *Management Today*.

Time was when most large U.S. manufacturers owned all the elements of their business systems—right back to the source of raw materials for their products or components. But keeping all operations under one roof can result in profitable areas subsidizing the less efficient, and that's no way to run a business in a highly competitive world. The author describes how many U.S. manufacturers are disintegrating—dismantling their farflung organizations and concentrating on core activities, in a way that may set the trend for manufacturing industry worldwide.

The classic structure of multinational corporations is in the middle of the greatest sea-change since World War II. The ultimate destination of this rapid evolution is far from clear, but the old mold, the old managerial assumptions and the old global strategies are fast disintegrating. One characteristic that is becoming obsolete is vertical integration—corporate behemoths which own and control nearly all the factors of production.

Henry Ford had a sheep farm that grew wool for car seat covers. The old General Motors-DuPont combination made car paint. Press lords owned both paper mills and forests. No self-respecting tire company was without its own rubber plantations. Copper and aluminum producers were also big fabricators. In short, it was an axiom that the more a firm controlled all the ingredients of manufacture and sale, the greater its consequent prosperity.

Today, however, that old shibboleth is the mark of the dinosaur. For more than a decade, vertical integration has been losing luster as a goal in the large multinationals. Some of them have been trimming back. Publishing empires like Time, Inc. disengaged themselves from paper and pulp making; nonferrous metals outfits moved out of fabrication; in steel, mini-mills have beaten the pants off the big integrated producers like U.S. Steel and Bethlehem; many food companies have left the agribusiness.

But lately this unravelling of the old vertical integration has greatly intensified, largely on account of new patterns of global competition, the speed of technological change and shorter product life-cycles. Also playing a part are volatile and unpredictable shifts in currency exchange values and the insuperable task of managing vast corporate empires. "Companies always used to think, 'Our people can manage their way out of the problems of size and complexity.' But the evidence is that they

John Thackray, "America's Vertical Cutback," *Management Today* (June 1986) 74–76, 94. Copyright © 1986 by Management Publications Ltd. Reprinted by permission.

can't," notes Steven C. Wheelwright, professor at the Stanford University Graduate School of Business.

## Dynamic Networks

"Disaggregation" or "disintegration" is now the name of the game: a process which seeks competitive advantage by focusing corporate energies and resources only on those factors of production and/or distribution in which there's an edge, and renouncing the rest. In today's fiercely competitive climate, a corporation cannot afford to do battle on any field where it doesn't wield the strongest weapons or wear the thickest armor. No longer can it hope that economies and efficiencies in one facet of production—say, low raw material costs, or superior distribution channels—can subsidize those processes where it's a high-cost operator.

So what's emerging is the ad hoc, pragmatic and impromptu company that lives according to no grand design. And with this change has come a new spirit of organizational experimentation and a groping for new forms and identities. "Our business is one of relationships," says a top executive of Galoob, a toy company that coordinates outside inventors, design specialists, factories, packagers, manufacturers' reps and finance companies.

Raymond E. Miles, dean of the School of Business Administration at the University of California at Berkeley, has dubbed this prototypical corporation a "dynamic network."* What he sees emerging is "a switchboard instead of a corporation." Another term, preferred by Michael J. Piore and Charles F. Sabel, authors of *The Second Industrial Divide,* is "flexible specialization."

Non-integration isn't new in business, of course. It has been characteristic of the garment trade, of publishing, of construction—where much production is traditionally farmed out. What's new, and what might ultimately cause massive dislocation in the entire industrialized and semi-industrialized world, is that most of the world's big manufacturing and selling outfits are following suit; through joint ventures, R&D sharing, production-distribution partnerships and offshore sourcing agreements in such key industries as cars, machine tools, video recorders, industrial robots, optics, consumer appliances and medical equipment.

Ineluctably, the world's advanced economies are being restructured by this breakup of vertical integration. "American companies are realizing that, to control the critical steps in a business system, you don't necessarily have to own them yourself," says Quincy J. Hunsicker, a director of the McKinsey consulting firm.

## Dangers in Partnership

How much control over events the various parties to these novel alliances actually have in the long run is the subject of an intense debate, involving as it does major

---

* See "Network organizations: new concepts for new forms" on page 53 of this issue.

shifts in employment around the world. General Electric spent $1.4 billion last year on offshore sourcing of products it sells under the company label. GE, which in 1980 had the leading market share in microwave ovens, now no longer manufactures them at all. It's the same for color TV. Next year GE will go offshore for its entire supply of room air conditioners. "With technology changing so quickly, you may not necessarily want to tie yourself down to making some piece of a product or providing a service—you may want to let it rest with a specialist," shrugs Fred W. Garry, a vice president for corporate engineering at General Electric.

The danger which sometimes follows is that the specialist might wax strong and become a threat along all dimensions of production and distribution. The sharing of technology is often a short-term romance. In a study of 100 recent joint ventures between American and Japanese companies, Eric Mankin and Robert B. Reich found that the Japanese partner got the technology infusion from the U.S. partner, which benefited from this cheap source of financing. Subsequently, the Japanese took over the advanced manufacturing role, leaving the American with—at most—low-tech assembly, sales and distribution in the United States.

Concrete examples of this are numerous. Kawasaki Heavy Industries now dominates in robots, where once its U.S. partner, Unimation, was kingpin. 3M markets a plain-paper copier manufactured by Toshiba, but Toshiba (under its own brand name) is undercutting 3M's prices by a fifth. Bell & Howell had a sweet-sharing deal with Canon in the 1960s, selling the products of the Japanese camera maker. But when Canon got hungry for a larger market share, Bell & Howell was thrown over. RCA once had a monopoly on color TV technology; it sold the knowhow to the Japanese and brought considerable strategic damage to itself.

## Squandering Resources

But in these sharing decisions, the U.S. players may not have much freedom of choice—given the ready availability of technology for sale and of competing distributors. Many sharing partnerships represent an intelligent decision to maximize returns on technological knowledge or market share. What the critics of this sharing sometimes fail to weigh is the huge waste of U.S. assets by companies that have gone the opposite route and invested heavily to become as low-cost as the Japanese, often with a strong dose of automation: but have still failed.

McKinsey's Elizabeth Haas tells the story of an industrial products company in the Mid-West which tried to improve manufacturing efficiency in an industry beset with overcapacity. A huge plant renovation program was launched; workers accepted stiff wage and benefit cuts; two layers of superfluous management were excised; fundamental product changes were made and equipment upgraded to modern standards.

"It was a remarkable effort," she says. "But it was not good enough. Volume kept dropping, because costs were too high relative to competitors." After much pain and suffering, the company's market share declined to almost nothing, and it got out of the business entirely. "A sinister logic confronts our manufacturers," she concludes. "Forced to combat low-cost foreign producers, they automate, school themselves in Japanese technology, integrate their operations with the help of computers and yet thereby increase the capacity of current facilities—frequently in an industry already burdened with idle plants."

Earlier this year there was a milestone event in the U.S. fork-lift truck industry: the last domestic producer, Clark Equipment, announced that it will shift all of its manufacturing to either South Korea or Brazil. (Rivals Caterpillar, Hyster and Yale moved offshore years ago.) Clark valiantly tried to improve its U.S. costs in much the same ways as in the example above, but its offshore competitors quickly went one better and remorselessly lowered prices. Only a year ago, Clark affirmed its commitment to U.S. manufacture—believing in part that its geographical proximity to the big U.S. market would improve its service capabilities and help with efficient lines of communications to customers. But these geographical pluses proved inadequate. "We also wanted to preserve a U.S. manufacturing base for the firm and for the nation."

## Manufacturing Shift _____

But the nation, or at least the Reagan Administration, seems unwilling to address this persistent erosion of its industrial base and manufacturing skills—despite strong commitment to improving national defense. Consequently, such classic "Buy America" integrated companies as Xerox, IBM and Motorola are far from being the self-sufficient empires they were a decade ago. Roughly two million people are employed worldwide in offshore assembly for U.S. and European firms. Offshore assembly has grown from 4 percent of U.S. imports in the early 1960s to around 10 percent currently—most of this being cars and parts, semiconductors, TV receivers and parts, office machines and clothing.

> *"You're seeing a substantial deindustrialization of the United States. And I can't imagine any country maintaining its position in the world without an industrial base," says Robert A. Lutz, a top Ford executive. Echoing the same point of view, Sony Corp.'s chairman and co-founder Akio Morita has famously declared that: "There's been a hollowing of American industry. The United States is abandoning its status as an industrial power."*

If so, there's money to be made in this abandonment—although perhaps only in the short term. "The value added in consumer electronics is in marketing, sales and distribution—not manufacturing," argues GE vice president Jacques A. Robinson, adding that "since you're working your capital harder, the return on investment goes up noticeably." In the bicycle business, "the leverage is no longer in manufacturing," observes Schwinn Bicycle Co.'s president, Edward R. Schwinn; so this company designs, distributes and merchandises only. Likewise, although RCA never did adequately solve the problem of making its own domestic video cassette recorders, it has reaped lush profits as a marketer of the Japanese-made product.

## Too Little, Too Late?

The trouble with this global division of functions, say the critics, is that the various factors of production and distribution cannot be picked up and discarded like cards in a game of gin rummy. When a machine tool builder like Cincinnati Milacron throws in the manufacturing towel and becomes merely an outlet for lower-cost Japanese production, it promises to become a pauper. "The thing that makes offshore production so dangerous is that it puts you in the mentality of letting the other guy do the hard stuff," says Harvard Business School professor Robert Hayes. "When the other guy enters the market, he's worked with the process on a daily basis, has a sense of the wider potential of the technology, of possible applications that you wouldn't have been thinking about. He's got all the advantages. Eventually, he who can do nothing but sell is at a great disadvantage."

Maybe so. But in many industries, the moment when corrective measures could have been taken has come and gone. A McKinsey study of the U.S. construction equipment business, for example, found that many U.S. firms have been operating at a cost disadvantage of 30 to 55 percent and are losing ground on productivity by a factor of two to one. A Booz·Allen & Hamilton study of the machined forgings industry turned up an equally grave cost gap, with producers from South Korea, Brazil and India rapidly gaining market share.

To be sure, some of the domestic manufacturers' disadvantage lay in the overvalued dollar. But according to B. Charles Ames, the chief of Acme-Cleveland Corp., the fault also lies with old and obsolete plants, excessive wages and benefits, "a manufacturing process that chews up working capital beyond sensible guidelines—i.e., 35 cents of receivables and FIFO inventories per dollar of sales—plus structured costs built up during the years when automatic price increases covered indiscriminate staff additions."

## From Multinational to Transnational

Curing these problems when demand is flat, prices are falling and there's world excess capacity in most industrial products is a challenge few chief executives have either the wisdom or the energy to undertake. "Most of them give lip-service to the problems of inefficient manufacture. Six out of seven of the 50 companies we studied think the nation has a problem but *their* company doesn't. They appear to be basing their confidence on hope, because they often don't know their competitors' manufacturing costs," comments Steven Walleck, a McKinsey director.

The logic of this McKinsey research is that, in the displacement of the U.S. manufacturing base, you ain't seen nothing yet. The rust in the Rust Bowl is swiftly eating away at the metal within. As the likes of Caterpillar Tractor, Cummins Engine and FMC move toward sourcing a third of their forging purchases from abroad, versus almost none five years ago, the U.S. domestic supplier base will face a crisis of survival. Those U.S. forging suppliers which thought they would always have a geopolitical leg-up, because of their short lines of communications, more easily accessed inventories, historical relationships and common language, are being proven quite wrong—at least when it comes to products with long production runs.

There is another tide running against them. Purchasing agents in the big buyer firms have been busy whittling down the numbers of their suppliers—which means that the small and innovative operator probably can't get an audience. Since 1981, Ford Motor has trimmed the number of its North American suppliers by 30 percent.

This sweeping tide of globalism will force vast prospective changes in the multinational firm. The autonomy of local subsidiaries, so long an object of management pride, must be curbed when total systems of production and distribution are the dominant organizational form. Indeed, the likelihood is that many of the multinationals' higher-cost outposts will have to be scrapped in favor of more centralized patterns of financing, research, manufacture and global distribution. "Economic realities are thus forcing the multinational to become a transnational system," management guru Peter Drucker observes.

## "Global" Initiatives _____

And yet in all major countries the political environment in which every business has to operate is becoming more nationalist, more protectionist—indeed, more chauvinistic—day by day. But Drucker believes that the multinational really has little choice. "If it fails to adjust to transnational economic reality, it will fast become inefficient and uneconomical."

Only a violent out-and-out trade war could spoil Drucker's prediction and break up all the new patterns of alliance, joint venture and mutual interdependence, now sprouting like mushrooms after summer rain. But naturally, too, the more this process evolves, giving consumers everywhere real benefits of competitive intensity, the harder it will be to halt. There is a symbiosis between the United States and the other industrialized and newly industrialized nations, which is nothing but an extreme application of Adam Smith's free-trade doctrine of comparative advantage.

Why shouldn't Kodak buy video cassette recorders and video tape and mid-size copying machines from Japan, or Detroit import a third of the contents of its cars? Why shouldn't IBM buy parts for its personal computer abroad, or U.S. industry be dependent on foreign sources for three-quarters of its miniature bearings? So Adam Smith might well wonder, were he still alive today.

The only foreseeable alternatives are political barriers that would diminish competitiveness and inflate end-product costs. Even if it turns out that the critics of the new disaggregation are right, in the sense that the process entails an enfeebling of vital industrial juices, the remedy is clear: the United States must fund a moon-shot style research and development effort that will make its factories the most efficient and productive in the world.

What's more, the drain isn't all one-sided. Here and there, thanks to the accelerating technologies of automation and flexible manufacturing, the pendulum has swung the other way. Japan, for instance, has lately pulled back many of its electronics investments in other Pacific Rim countries in favor of highly automated production at home. Some of the same opportunities exist in the United States. Last year Fairchild Camera & Instrument, owned by Schlumberger, shifted the welding of semiconductor chips to frames from a manual operation in Singapore and Indonesia into a state-of-the-art automated plant in Portland, Maine.

Not only are output costs more favorable at the new plant, but its location offers a new responsiveness to customers' service needs. "The rise in the use of automated equipment is rapidly dispelling the advantages that used to exist for assembly in Asia," says Robert M. Clary, an electronics consultant with Rose Associates of Los Altos, California.

## All-Round Benefits

So the pattern that is most likely to emerge will be a fluid one: where superior components of production exist abroad, the capital will follow. This is no more than part and parcel of "the diffusion of power away from the United States and the Soviet Union, which for 20 years has been the underlying pattern on the world scene," according to W. W. Rostow, formerly special assistant to President Kennedy for national security affairs.

But thanks to the speed of technological change, market shifts and consumer preferences, there will always be a countervailing tide. Witness the huge inflow of Japanese direct investment to the United States recently: some of it toward manufacturing the very items that U.S. corporations have sourced offshore—like compact cars and TV sets and semiconductors—which could very likely have a ripple effect and introduce more competitive practices to North America. There are now more than 300 Japanese-owned manufacturing plants in the United States, which between them employ some 50,000 people.

Cross-border partnering is the 1980s' contribution to global efficiency. "It is no longer a question of whether to pursue alliances, but how and when," notes McKinsey's Kenichi Ohmae. "Consortia will be the key to many companies' success. Managers must become nimble and skillful at leveraging their core talents in key markets around the world. And they will have to develop the skills to supplant their own weaknesses with other companies' strengths."

When they find and apply these skills, society as a whole may benefit. Some years ago, for example, Firestone Tire was deep in the red trying to make truck radial tires. It sold this factory to Japan's Bridgestone Corp., which soon became Firestone's radial truck tire supplier. As a marketer of this product, Firestone is quite profitable. Assuming that Bridgestone is, too, then the health and longevity of that asset have been improved by this deal. "More and more companies are saying it is not required that you manufacture a product if you need to continue to market it," says John J. Nevin, chairman of Firestone.

## Strategic Partnering

Beset with overcapacity, integrated steel producers are an obvious theater for strategic partnering: because of the pressing need to rationalize this industry. Thus in Europe there's been an alliance between Luxembourg's Arbed and Belgium's Cockerill-Sambre to exchange different product types via a supply contract, permitting both companies to shut down uneconomic plant.

Similarly, California Steel (formerly owned and unprofitably run by Kaiser Steel) gets slabs from Brazil's Tubarao plant at far lower cost than Kaiser's facility could achieve. "Competition is more likely to be strengthened by such alliances than weakened," says McKinsey's Eric G. Friberg. "Strategic alliances between two companies not competing today that give both concerns access to more modern, productive facilities can lead only to lower costs and more aggressive competition."

Olivetti and AT&T; Sony selling RCA satellites in Japan; Rolls-Royce-Kawasaki-Pratt-Whitney; Hitachi and Hewlett-Packard; ICL-Fujitsu-Amdahl-Siemens; Westinghouse and Toshiba; General Motors and Toyota—this proliferation of cooperative deals lying side by side with fierce competition could eventually alter the industrial map of the world. Big and powerful though corporations like the above have become, they cannot keep up with the expanding scale and the heightened competitiveness of world markets. They face scarcity of resources and increased risk from a volatile environment. So the new partnering expresses a kind of devolution of the global factors of production into the stronger hands. Such radical change is bound to be disruptive and to favor some at the expense of others, notably highly paid factory workers in the United States and Europe.

## Boeing Bites the Bullet _____

No nation, far less any corporation, can these days long sustain a total dominance in any global product. The very last industry where the United States had undisputed ascendancy, commercial jet aircraft, has lately bowed to the logic of global partnering. Earlier this year, Boeing declared that it would cooperate with a consortium of Japanese aerospace firms in the projected $4 billion development of the 7J7, one of the new generation of fuel-efficient turbo-prop aircraft.

Japan's Ministry of International Trade and Industry has, of course, targeted jet transport, along with computers and telecommunications gear, as a primary strategic goal for the nation's industrial future. The deal with Boeing will give the Japanese industry a major foot in the door, plus a share of the production and profits, in return for bearing 25 percent of the cost.

Critics of this landmark technological transfer argue that Boeing shouldn't squander its experience and its standing as the only profitable airframe maker in the United States, and jeopardize the nation's most successful export—worth a $4.5 billion trade surplus in 1985. "Let's not give away the family jewels," is the typical response of Robert B. Reich, a prominent Democratic Party intellectual and teacher at Harvard's John F. Kennedy School of Government.

But Boeing's management sees the world from a very different angle. First of all, "Multinational involvements such as joint ventures and consortia have become a fact of life in recent years among major commercial aircraft and engine producers," according to Thomas J. Bacher, director of international business and government affairs at Boeing. In fact, he argues, life would be impossible without tradeoffs of market access, low-cost financing and jobs. Japanese and Italian firms are currently part of the Boeing 767 program, "under an arrangement that involves substantial risk sharing," he points out.

Then, too, Airbus Industrie's recent market successes and rising political clout need to be checked: quite likely Boeing brass was deathly scared that the Japanese would team up with Airbus, as well they might have. In the final analysis, moreover, the Japanese are just too powerful and resourceful to be thwarted. "The risk of creating a new independent competitor appears minimal," Bacher feels. "But it is probably unavoidable in any case, should Japan seek such a role."

## Reduced Vulnerability _____

The Boeing-Japan hook-up demonstrates that the patterns of sharing—the cross licensing, sales agents, R&D liaison, market cooperation, etc.—have moved from being marginal and episodic to a central role on the global stage, and the core of corporate strategies.

In reality, for a major corporation to seek to control all the factors of production and distribution is to invite vulnerabilities today. By the same logic, U.S. corporations no longer build mammoth plants, but have significantly downsized facilities to reduce their exposure to socioeconomic change and volatilities. General Electric's aircraft engines, which used to be manufactured in two massive facilities, are now made in eight satellite plants. Plants built in the United States before 1970 had on average 644 employees; those planned for the 1980s should have no more than 210 people—a two-thirds reduction which is an apt measure of the turbulent conditions today.

The pan-national corporation whose outline is now taking shape will not be easy to control. "There are many supply-chain costs and problems in working out an international sourcing strategy," says Booz·Allen & Hamilton consultant and vice president Robert Meyer. "From time to time the links in the chain break down, and there's an immediate impact on costs and quality that can be very painful. It's the same problem Hannibal had going over the Alps." There are, in addition, numerous political risks in teaming up with less than stable newly industrialized countries like Brazil or South Korea.

Despite the birth pangs, it is clear that something wholly new and strange is beginning to emerge. The old-style multinational, whose products and services are replicated by factories and distribution systems in many countries, will not perish altogether. Nor will, in certain products, the entirely domestic corporation. World-scale competition simultaneously causes restructuring of manufacturing and distribution toward centralization and decentralization. Clearly, too, in some cases vertical integration will continue to prevail—oil and gas, steel and nonferrous metals, for instance. But gone forever are the familiar multinational patterns of the past—and, for management, the easy strategic choices departed with them.

# ANNOTATED BIBLIOGRAPHY

# ANNOTATED BIBLIOGRAPHY

Arai, Joyi. "The Success of the Japanese—Part I." *Production and Inventory Management Review* 1.12 (December 1981): 26–28.

*A well-planned and coordinated economic policy, involving the allocation of natural resources to those sectors where they would produce the highest value added, was necessary to set Japan back on her feet after World War II. Many factors contributed to the resultant productivity growth in the decades that followed. This article explores some of these major factors.*

Arai, Joyi. "The Success of the Japanese—Part II." *Production and Inventory Management Review* 2.1 (January 1982):26–28.

*Japan is a nation of paradoxes with many problems to overcome. Its recent productivity increases were only attained through a vigorous effort to eliminate waste of materials, energy, and human input. Management now faces the critical issue of maintaining its work force under the lifetime employment system while making the transition to a knowledge-intensive society, which requires fewer blue-collar workers.*

Baranson, Jack. *Robots in Manufacturing: Key to International Competitiveness.* (Lomond Publications, Inc., 1983), 168 pp.

*Though the book emphasizes "Robots" in its title, the reader will soon see that Baranson is really discussing "Automated Manufacturing Equipment and Systems" or AMES—which usually incorporates robots as part of the total system.*

Bartholdi, John J., III. "Operations Research in China." *Interfaces* 16.2 (March-April 1986): 24–30.

*Apparently the leaders of China intend to use management science and operations research to help modernize the country. However, the traditions of China, as well as its recent past, make the effective application of MS/OR problematic.*

Chung, Byung Soo, and Chung H. Lee. "The Choice of Production Techniques by Foreign and Local Firms in Korea." *Economic Development and Cultural Change* 29.1 (October 1980):135–40.

*In this paper, the authors investigate the production techniques used by U.S. and Japanese subsidiaries in Korea, on the one hand, and those used by their local counterparts in the same industries, on the other.*

Contractor, Farok J. *International Technology Licensing: Compensation, Costs, and Negotiation.* (Lexington, Mass.: Lexington Books, 1981), 193 pp.

*The book is a "state of the art" summary of licensing issues and practices which provide useful comparisons among strategies and policies of a limited number of U.S. firms.*

Cooper, Carl. "The Japanese Connection: Imitate or Emulate?" *Production and Inventory Management* (Third Quarter 1984): 114–25.

*Much has been written about Japanese success in the international marketplace. This article provides an overview of Japanese culture, the resultant business and management practices, and indicates some concern for its future survival. It is meant to stimulate the reader to evaluate effectively the methodologies in light of existing American cultural norms in order to help formulate strategies for the future.*

Dale, B. G., J. L. Burbidge, and M. J. Cottam. "Planning the Introduction of Group Technology." *International Journal of Operations Production and Management* 4.1 (1984): 34–47.

*A large multinational engineering company with production facilities in the UK recently undertook a study in the possibility of using group technology in a proposed "focused factory" for the manufacture of transmission gears and shafts. This paper briefly describes the reasons for considering this type of change. It also describes the method used to predict the likely benefits in comparison with conventional forms of organization, and to plan the machine groups and part families for group technology.*

Dale, B. G., and A. J. Duncalf. "Quality-Related Decision Making: A Study in Six British Companies." *International Journal of Operations Production and Management* 5.1 (1985): 15–25.

*This article presents the results of a study on how quality-related decisions are made in six case study companies. The investigation in each company involved interviews with selected members of the management team, particularly those involved in quality-related decision making. The interviews were conducted in two parts: the first part followed a structured interview approach, while the second part involved an unstructured discussion. The work reveals that companies, without a formulated quality management policy and where the chief executive does not take the lead in the management of quality, are unlikely to be able to coordinate effectively their quality-related decision making, and, consequently, their approach to quality tends to be inspection oriented. It also points out that the involvement of quality staff in design, purchasing, and market feedback is vital, since it ensures that quality-related decision making is effective and consistent with management policy.*

Dale, B. G., and J. Lee. "Factors Which Influence the Success of Quality Circle Programmes in the United Kingdom." *International Journal of Operations Production and Management* 5.4 (1985): 43–54.

*This article presents an analysis of quality circle data gathered by questionnaire and which is used to classify whether a programme has been a success, failure, or is just surviving. The findings reveal few black-and-white differences between the three categories. It is pointed out that factors typically outlined in circle literature as essential for success are helpful in some organizations, but not in others, and in some cases can be positive detractors. Factors emerging as more critical to success include how well members of each circle work together, the extent to which an organization has a total approach to quality and a good understanding of the philosophy and disciplines of quality management. What constitutes a success, survivor, or failure is also questioned, and some suggestions for a more accurate definition are advanced.*

Davis, Harold S. "Management: What We Can Learn from the Japanese." *Production and Inventory Management* 27.1 (First Quarter 1986): 85–89.

*If productivity is to be increased, effective managers must find ways to maximize what their labor force can produce. This article shows how the Japanese have accomplished this and explains which of their procedures we might emulate.*

Dequan, Chen, Ji Lei, and Pang Chungmin. "Popularization of Management in China." *Interfaces* 16.2 (March-April 1986): 2–9.

*Since the early 1960s, China has been applying mathematical methods to production and planning problems in an environment where qualified personnel are scarce, and where computers are not readily available. Professor Hua Loo-Keng chose the path of popularization, selecting methods which do not require large and complex calculations, and which can be used by those with relatively little education. A large number of problems can be solved using fairly simple mathematical methods easily taught to nonspecialists. Popularization of mathematical methods has provided a way to extend the application and impact of management science in China.*

Dunning, John. *International Production and the Multinational Enterprise.* (London: George Allen and Unwin, 1981), 439 pp.

*This book gives an analysis on the "Eclectic Theory of International Production." It also deals with the impact of MNEs on the economies of host and home countries.*

Emmanuel, Arghin. *Appropriate or Underdeveloped Technology?* (New York: John Wiley and Sons, Inc., 1982), 186 pp.

*This provocative work questions many of today's views on technology transfer. It asserts that "appropriate" technology, tailor-made for the needs of developing countries, merely widens the gap between the developing and the developed countries.*

Finch, Byron. "Japanese Management Techniques in Small Manufacturing Companies: A Strategy for Implementation." *Production and Inventory Management* 27.3 (Third Quarter 1986): 30–38.

*Just-in-time production techniques have been implemented in many large U.S. companies; however, little information is available on their suitability in small manufacturing companies. This article presents the unique problems that could be expected by the small manufacturer, and offers an implementation strategy to minimize the severity of these problems.*

Frame, Davidson. *International Business and Global Technology.* (Lexington, Mass.: D.C. Heath and Company, 1983), 224 pp.

*This book focuses on two major forces that shape the character of our modern world: the growth of international business and the rapid development in science and technology.*

Garson, David G. *Workers Self-Management in Industry: The West European Experience.* (New York: Praeger, 1977), 230 pp.

*Self-management is increasing throughout Western Europe, and governments are becoming more receptive to it because they see it as a means toward greater economic productivity.*

Goonatilake, P. C. L. "Inventory Control Problems in Developing Countries." *International Journal of Operations Production and Management* 4.4 (1984): 57–64.

*This article examines inventory control problems in developing countries using the results of a field study conducted in the industrial sector for a developing country. It is shown that ineffective inventory control is a major problem faced by industries in developing countries, and that even the very basic inventory control concepts and techniques are not used by the majority of the companies studied. Due to the heavy reliance on imported industrial raw materials and parts, and the endemic bureaucratic delays and associated communication problems in developing countries, order lead times cannot be computed with any degree of accuracy; therefore, manufacturers attempt to overcome the uncertainty by carrying excessive amounts of buffer stocks.*

Gordon, John R. M., and Peter R. Richardson. "Measuring Total Manufacturing Performance." *Sloan Management Review* 21.2 (Winter 1980): 47–58.

*This paper presents findings from the authors' research in samples of Canadian manufacturing companies. The authors contend that productivity measures which compare output to input, compare only one dimension in the evaluation of manufacturing performance.*

Gordon, Ronald G., and E. Robert Ross. "Expanding Sourcing and Distributing Functions Internationally." *Production and Inventory Management Review* 1.5 (May 1981): 25–26.

*This article has not attempted to cover all aspects of establishing or expanding sourcing and distribution functions on an international basis, but should provide some insight into the basic guidelines for recognizing and investigating increased operations in a worldwide marketplace.*

Graves, Stephen C. "Reflections on Operations Management in Shanghai." *Interfaces* 16.2 (March-April 1986): 10–17.

*In supervising student projects with local enterprises in Shanghai, the author found that the foci of the projects were, for the most part, to study an operation and to determine how to improve it. In this respect the projects were no different from those in the West. But the projects did differ in terms of objectives, constraints, and because computing technology was less available. Three projects illustrate the types of studies conducted.*

Harvey, Robert E. "Is Japan Doing a Better Job Managing Inventory?" *Iron Age* 224.16 (June 1, 1981): 38–42.

*This article examines the inventory system of Japanese companies.*

Hayes, Robert H. "Why Japanese Factories Work." *Harvard Business Review* (July-August 1981): 56–66.

*Japanese managers have achieved their phenomenal manufacturing services, says Robert Hayes, not by using advanced technologies and fashionable management techniques, but by paying close attention to the basics. Never complacent, they continue to work toward flawless factory operations and perfect products.*

Henzler, Herbert, and Wilhelm Rall. "Facing Up to the Globalization Challenge." *The McKinsey Quarterly* (Winter 1976): 52–68.

*When in industry after industry companies are gearing up to "go global," any business that hesitates too long—or fails altogether to respond—risks economic jeopardy, the authors argue. Here, with a particular eye to the European business environment, they propose how top management might assess the opportunities and their company's ability to implement the strategies involved, develop action programs based on a realistic assessment of the company's strengths and weaknesses, and put in place the organization needed for operating on the appropriate chosen scale.*

Kanter, Rosabeth Moss. *The Change Masters: Innovations for Productivity in The American Corporation.* (New York: Simon and Schuster, 1983), 432 pp.

The theme of *The Change Masters* is deceptively simple: Times have changed. People at all levels of the organization must be actively and meaningfully involved in productivity improvement.

Kawada, Hisashi, and Soloman B. Levine. *Human Resources in Japanese Industrial Development.* (Princeton, N.J.: Princeton University Press, 1980), 322 pp.

*Levine and Kawada examine the role of human skills in the Japanese economy in this field of study.*

Kim, Chan W. "Global Production Sharing: An Empirical Investigation of the Pacific Electronics Industry." *Management International Review* 26.2 (1986): 62–70.

*The most obvious manifestation of global production sharing is the growth of intermediate product trade within the Pacific electronics industry. This paper empirically reveals the pattern of global production sharing in the Pacific electronics industry where Japan exports to the United States through the Asian Newly Industrialized Countries (ANICs) by supplying intermediate products to the ANICs, which are then incorporated into finished products destined for the United States. Findings suggest that global production sharing can serve as a strategic route to organize the operations of manufacturing firms in the face of increasing global competition and a rising tide of protectionism.*

Kim, Jae Won. "CES Production Functions in Manufacturing, and Problems of Industrialization in LDCs: Evidence from Korea." *Economic Development and Cultural Change* 33.1 (October 1984): 143–66.

*The author discusses CES production functions for two-digit industries in Korea. One purpose is to show empirically that the elasticities of substitution are not zero in almost all of Korea's industries regardless of the firm's size. The author also shows that production functions differ across different sized groups of business firms in a given industry.*

Kivijarvi, Hannu, Pekka Korhonen, and Jurki Wallenius. "Operations Research and Its Practices in Finland." *Interfaces* 16.4 (July-August 1986): 53–59.

*A survey of sixty-four private and government organizations in Finland revealed that they used over 150 different operations research models. Academic operations research was reviewed on the basis of published reports, interviews with representatives of university departments, and personal observations. Considerable activity exists to promote the theory and practice of management science/operations research in industry, in the public sector, and in several universities.*

Kumar, G. Surya. "Improving Material Productivity." *Production and Inventory Management Review* 5.4 (April 1985): 52–56.

*A casual trip through the locomotive manufacturing plant floor revealed scrap heaps of assorted sizes and shapes of steel.*

Lincoln, James R., Mitsuyo Handa, and Kerry McBride. "Organizational Structures in Japanese and U.S. Manufacturing." *Administrative Science Quarterly* 31.3 (1986): 338–64.

*They report the findings of a comparative survey of fifty-five American and fifty-one Japanese manufacturing plants, focusing on differences in organizational structures and the influences of task environment and other determining variables on those structures. Significant differences in structural characteristics include less specialization, taller hierarchies, greater formal centralization, but less de facto centralization in the Japanese organizations. The effects of operations technology on the structuring of plants were also found to be weaker in Japan than in the United States, a pattern anticipated from the premise that Japanese organizations are embedded in a tighter institutional environment than U.S. organizations. The study also gave some support for the speculative thesis of parallels between Japanese organization and modes of organizing associated with advanced production technology.*

McInnes, J. M. Corporate Management of Productivity—An Empirical Study." *Strategic Management Journal* 5.4 (October-December 1984): 351–65.

*This article provides an analysis that compares and contrasts managerial approaches to productivity among the American, British, and Japanese samples of companies.*

McMillan, Charles J. "Production Planning and Organization Design at Toyota." *Business Quarterly* (Winter 1981): 22–30.

*Toyota alone produced more cars than the entire U.K. auto industry, and the Japanese have overtaken the French in Francophone Africa. Japan's system of production planning and organizational design has an important bearing on this success.*

Munchus, George, III. "Collective Bargaining and the Multinational Firm: Management Policy Issue for the Automobile Industry." *International Journal of Operations and Production Management* 5.1 (1985): 39–48.

*Although there has been a recent surge in adoption of the multinational corporation by the business community, a similar tendency is not evidenced by labour. This disparity can be attributed to limited resources, legal constraints, differences between countries, and economic inequalities. It can also be traced to the fact that while multinational corporations usually have defined objectives and means for their accomplishment, the international labour movement has been plagued by diverse political philosophies, varied bargaining tactics and strategies, power confrontations, and a slowness in specifying unified goals.*

*The purpose of this article is to examine the need, if one exists, to bargain on an international basis because of the growth of the multinational corporation. It will examine the alternatives available on the international scene with an emphasis on the role of the American union and the reactions its activities may generate. Because of the breadth of this topic and the wide range of effects various constraints may have on different industries, the auto industry will be addressed for purposes of example.*

Murphy, Kathleen. *Macroproject Development in the Third World: An Analysis of Transnational Partnerships.* (Boulder, CO: Westview Press, Inc., 1983), 196 pp.

*During the 1970s an unprecedented number of large-scale projects of various kinds were launched in the Third World. Many multinational corporations that were experienced in initiating such projects in industrialized nations encountered unanticipated difficulties and risks in the new settings. This book assesses the experiences of multinationals and host nations, and offers guidelines for effectively implementing macroprojects in developing areas.*

Nellemann, David O., CPIM, and Leighton F. Smith. "Just-in-Time vs. Just-in-Case: Production/Inventory Systems, Concepts Borrowed Back from Japan." *Production and Inventory Management* (Second Quarter 1982):12–21.

*Years of consulting experience in Japan provide the basis for this overview of efficient Japanese production and inventory systems concepts, including: The Roots of Japanese Productivity; The Just-in-Time Concept; Achieving a Uniform Flow; Group Technology and Production-Flow Systems. Particular emphasis focuses on the successful Japanese techniques applicable to American industry.*

Novitsky, Michael P., CPIM. "Lessons from Europe: What's Going on Across the Atlantic." *Production and Inventory Management Review* 5.4 (April 1985): 42–51.

*Because of the competitive pressures facing most manufacturing firms in Western Europe, many companies are mandating that major improvements be installed quickly throughout the entire logistics network.*

Nwachukwu, J. C. "Quality Control Practice in Developing Countries: The Case of Nigeria." *Management International Review* 25.4 (1985): 73–78.

*This paper presents the results of a study into the current quality control practice in Nigerian industries. One–hundred–and–two companies were involved in the study. The results showed that the manufacturing organizations in general have problems of quality control, which include among others: inadequate plant maintenance, lack of skilled operators and inspectors, and the virtual absence of metrological equipment. The results also revealed that many of the companies are not in a position to control all three facets of quality: design quality, manufacture quality, and quality of performance. Only the second facet is within the control of the indigenous Nigerian manufacturer. It is, therefore, imperative that the directions to improve the quality of locally manufactured goods should be toward the other two aspects.*

Papageorgiou, John C. "Management Science/Operations Research in Greece." *Interfaces* 16.4 (July-August 1986): 24–30.

*Management science/operations research has followed different patterns of growth in different countries depending on a number of factors, some of which relate to the uniqueness of the socioeconomic and cultural environment. In this paper the evolution of MS/OR in Greece and the results of a study conducted in 1977 aiming at finding the extent of MS/OR applications in the country are reviewed. Indicators of MS/OR work carried out in Greece are the papers presented at the annual national meetings of the Hellenic Operations Research Society and those papers that were presented in the first four annual meetings and were MS/OR related are summarized. Finally, the current status of MS/OR in Greece as perceived by the author during his visit to Greece is evaluated.*

Plenert, Gerhard. "Are Japanese Production Methods Applicable in the United States?" *Production and Inventory Management* (Second Quarter 1985): 121–29.

*Research was performed to analyze all the differences between the U.S. MRP and the Japanese JIT environments. A selection of Japanese techniques that seem appropriate for adoption in the United States is described.*

Plossl, George W. "Japanese Productivity: Myth vs. Reality." *Production and Inventory Management Review* 9 (September 1981): 59–62.

*Businesspersons in escalating numbers have visited Japan, returning with "expert" opinions on how they did it. Inevitable myths appeared and spread, fueled by the frustrations of those yearning for simple solutions, basic misunderstandings by casual observers, and cynics seeking to explain their own failures.*

Poh, Khong Heng. "NC Applications—Its Present and Future in Singapore's Industries." *International Journal of Operations and Production Management* 4.1 (1984): 12–17.

*The numerically controlled machine tool has become a very topical subject due to the current emphasis on increasing productivity and upgrading of the manufacturing industry. This paper reviews the current applications of NC machine tools in Singapore. It also takes a look at the future directions in which NC is likely to develop, particularly in the area of computer-aided manufacture, and examines the role of the production engineer within this new environment.*

Reid, Richard A., and Smith, Howard L. "Concepts Underlying Japanese Management." *Journal of Purchasing and Materials Management* (Winter 1983): 14–20.

*The purpose of this article is to explore the concepts underlying Japanese management and to address their implications for purchasing and materials managers.*

Rice, James W., and Takeo Yoshikawa. "MRP and Motovation: What Can We Learn From Japan?" *Production and Inventory Management* (Second Quarter 1980): 45–52.

*The authors provide an examination of the phenomenal increase of industrial production in Japan. They also examine the reasons for this rapid growth increase and examine the traditional system used by Japanese industry, which has lead to such spectacular economic growth.*

Ross, Ian M. "The Global Contest in Industrial Competitiveness Has Just Begun." *Research Management* XXVIII.3 (May-June 1985):10–14.

*More of the intellect and power of today's R & D should be applied to industrial innovation, particularly to production processes.*

Saint-Phalle, Thibaut de. *U.S. Productivity and Competitiveness in International Trade.* (Washington, D.C.: Center for Strategic and International Studies, Georgetown University, 1980), 117 pp.

*The book analyzes the current situations of twelve high-technology U.S. industries that have traditionally been world leaders in technological advances, and presents positive solutions to the productivity decline.*

Schonberger, Richard J. *Japanese Manufacturing Techniques: Nine Hidden Lessons in Simplicity.* (New York: The Free Press, 1982), 260 pp.

*Schonberger's book is a first-class exposition of what has been learned from Japanese production techniques.*

Siggel, Eckhard. "On The Nature of Technology Shelves Facing Less Developed Countries: Some Hypotheses and Case Studies." *The Journal of Developing Areas* (January 1984): 227–46.

*The main questions asked in this literature are: How much room for substitution among factors exists, to what extent are the techniques chosen socially optimal, and what are the determinants of technological choice?*

Sprague, Linda G., CPIM, and Hugh Thomas. "Lot-Sizing Methods in China." *Production and Inventory Management* (Second Quarter 1985): 105–14.

*The lot-sizing methods most commonly taught and practiced in Chinese factories are described. The smallest batch method is intended for use where there is demand volatility. The production interval method—the most widely used procedure—is intended for stable demand situations. Both methods operate in the context of a centrally planned Marxist economy.*

Takeuchi, Hirotaka. "Productivity: Learning from the Japanese." *California Management Review* XXIII.4 (Summer 1981): 5–19.

*Several companies in the United States have recently adopted productivity improvement programs which have long been implemented in Japan. The author analyzes the factors that have led to the success of Japanese programs, and describes how U.S. companies can establish and manage productivity systems.*

The Centre for Policy Studies. *Quality Control in a Developing Economy: A Case Study of Israel.* (Jerusalem, Israel: Keter Publishing House, 1970), 311 pages.

*This book attempts to present the problems of quality control in Israel and the policies required to improve the prevailing situation.*

Voss, C. A. "Japanese Manufacturing Management Practices in the U.K." *International Journal of Operations and Protection Management* 4.2 (1984): 31–38.

*Japan is perceived in most advanced countries as the world leader in the introduction and exploitation of new management practices, particularly in the area of manufacturing. In an attempt to match Japan's economic progress, other countries are seeking to introduce many of the systems that are believed to be the basis of Japanese success. In this article, certain aspects of a U.K. manufacturing company, which had adopted a number of practices following studies undertaken in Japan, is compared with a Japanese-owned company located in the United Kingdom.*

Wantuck, Kenneth A. "The ABC's of Japanese Productivity." *Production and Inventory Management Review* 1.9 (September 1981): 22–28.

*Japan has modified American production and inventory control techniques with amazing results. Some of the "secrets" of Japan's much-heralded productivity boom are actually long-established American methods shrouded in different terminology.*

Waters, C. D. J. "Is U.K. Manufacturing Industry Really Overstocked?" *International Journal of Physical Distribution and Materials Management* 14.5 (1984):5–10.

*It has been suggested that stock levels in this country are, as a whole, far too high. Some criticisms have attempted international comparisons and concluded that other industrial countries control their stocks more rigorously, thus reducing costs, increasing efficiency, and improving competitiveness. If these criticisms are justified, and stock levels are high in this country, it must either mean that U.K. industry is different in some way that makes higher stock levels necessary, or else British management is not using available methods of inventory control to the same extent as effectively as foreign managers. This article looks at these alternatives and considers related questions.*

Westring, Gosta. "Essential Elements of International Tendering." *International Trade Forum* 21.4 (October-December 1985): 4–9.

*Tendering is a fundamental aspect of the public procurement of goods and services. Some of the main features of the international tendering process are presented in this article.*

Whyback, D. Clay. "Production Planning and Control at Kumera Oy." *Production and Inventory Control* (First Quarter 1984): 71–82.

*This article presents the production planning and control system at the Kumera Company in Finland. The system, called periodic control, is a very simple but effective method for supporting "Game Plans" that are developed for the company as a whole. In this article a general manufacturing planning and control model is used to provide the framework for describing periodic control.*

Wild, Ray. "Survey Report: The Responsibilities and Activities of U.K. Production Managers." *International Journal of Operations and Production Management* 4.1 (1984): 69–74.

*A small and simple questionnaire survey of U.K. production managers was undertaken in 1983. The objective was to collect information to help in curriculum design. The summary results presented may be of interest to those who teach this subject. Data were collected from forty-five production managers (and those with a similar title) employed in manufacturing organizations. All respondents were engaged in the management of production in large, often multi-plant, companies.*

Wright, Mike, and David Rhodes. "Computerized Work Scheduling in a Not-for-Profit Service Organization: A Hospital Case Study." *International Journal of Operations and Production Management* 5.3 (1985): 39–52.

*Little attention has been paid in the literature to the introduction of computer–based production/work scheduling methods in not-for-profit organizations. This article redresses the balance using the case of the U.K. National Health Service as an illustration. The problems of control in this organization are discussed and a conceptually based approach to dealing with change in not-for-profit organizations is put forward. The conceptual discussion in the first half of the article is illustrated using the case study of the implementation of a computer-based work scheduling system in a high-*

*security hospital. The perceived need for the system, its details, problems in implemen-tation, the approach used in implementation, the effect on the organization, and re-maining issues are discussed. Finally, some general conclusions and recommendations are outlined.*